Walking on Water

A Path to Empowerment

REA NOLAN MARTIN

ISBN: 978-1532728204
LCCN: 2016906308

Available at Amazon.com

Visit www.ReaNolanMartin.com for more information.

"Everything you see has its roots in the unseen world.
The forms may change, yet the essence remains the same.
Every wonderful sight will vanish; every sweet word will fade,
But do not be disheartened,
The source they come from is eternal, growing,
Branching out, giving new life and new joy.
Why do you weep?
The source is within you
And this whole world is springing up from it."

— Rumi

contents

1

Getting Wet

L iving close to the Hudson River as I do, my family and I experienced 9/11 in ways unimaginable to the rest of the world or even the rest of the country. Stunned by the catastrophic impact of a diabolical plan hatched worlds away (both physically and philosophically), it took me years to fully understand the depth of its message. But as with most things, in the end the message was simple.

Wake up.

Shortly after that pristine September sky was saturated with death, New York's Mayor Giuliani asked everyone in the New York area to be on guard for suspicious behavior. We were told that our alertness would be critical to the safety of ourselves, our families, and our larger communities. The police couldn't be everywhere at once, he'd explained. "You are our eyes and ears."

This message did not go over well at first. Many were confused and frightened. *"What is he saying?! That it's up to us to stop planes from flying into buildings?!"* Some claimed that such an announcement was nothing short of a desperate cry of governmental ineptitude coupled with dangerous potential for widespread anxiety. Maybe so. After all, what could a single unarmed individual, or even group of individuals, possibly do in the face of committed evil?

It was time to find out.

This message eventually spread across our country to other countries in Europe and Asia. An awakening was afoot. And as with most unscheduled awakenings, those in the deepest slumber were cranky and resistant, if not enraged by the ear-splitting shriek of the physical alarm and the scorch of the apocalyptic light. Many Americans, shaken out of a deep sleep, dukes up, guns in hand, were driven to the kind of reactive posture produced by fear. But isn't fear what the enemy wants? Doesn't fear break us down even further? Can we name a single problem that fear has ever solved?

Though the timing of the cataclysm was decided by others, the choice to awaken was and remains ours. After all, this was not the only alarm. As 9/11 played out in the civilian arena, other travesties of our own design were occurring simultaneously in our neighborhoods, governments, schools, churches, ecology, and financial coliseums. The coma of perceived protection, material entitlement, and paternal authority was over.

Or maybe it was all an illusion to begin with.

I am not the only one who saw this seismic shift coming. Many mystics also did. Months prior to 9/11, a friend of mine and I had one confusing dream after another featuring violence schemed in mysterious Arab settings and executed in the U.S., complete with a dream of massive conflagrations at the tip of Manhattan.

Though we shared these stories with each other, we had no idea why we were dreaming them or what, if anything, could be done. As months passed into years and other events intervened, I understood better that this event was the crux of a world-changing cultural and philosophical shift whose impact would surge like a tidal wave of consciousness from shore to reluctant shore. Our prophetic dreams simply reflected the cosmic rise of that massive wave already in motion.

In Buddhism it is said that the enemy (which in this context can be a person or an event) is our best teacher. Unequivocally, 9/11 was mine. My sister suffered directly, though she survived. Like other survivors, she was inextricably changed, as were we all in varying degrees. Everyone in proximity was left with a hole blown through the regional and national looking glass, revealing the rage, poverty, fundamentalist beliefs, and crying need of distant desperate worlds. Worlds we would have happily avoided had we not been forced to look them in the eye.

In the end I think it will be written that this calamitous event triggered a rebirth, however savage the means. But don't most births involve hard labor, blood, and a degree or two of hardship and sacrifice? In this case it pitted man against man, society against society, belief against belief—even within our own country. We were finally forced to confront a reality that was and remains a systemic and pernicious disease in the human family. A disease we ignored until it landed like a missile in our own backyard. The thing about disease is—it can't be cured if it remains unobserved, undiagnosed and untreated.

There are benefits to facing the truth.

The ensuing decade of terror and breakdown formed a fragile bridge into a new world order (aka paradigm) of personal accountability and empowerment. No longer able to overlook either the victimhood

Understand the difference a single person can make.

or embedded evil of other shores, we were also forced to evaluate ourselves. What kind of people we were, not just domestically, but across all humanity. How we treated ourselves, our families, our neighbors, animals, and environment. How we treated the least of us—the handicapped, the mentally ill, and the impoverished. After all, we are all one deeply connected organism. Waking up to face our enemy, we learn something about ourselves. The point is not so much to judge the experience, but to "integrate the darkness into the light", as the great psychotherapist and visionary, Carl Jung, insisted was the only way forward.

We are not there yet.

These essays are intended, in a small way, to illuminate the path from personal victimhood to self-awareness and enablement that we are all charged to walk. Be awake; be aware. Understand the difference a single person can make. You. Me. One by one, we can learn to harness the divinity within to enlighten the world without. Equipped with that divinity, we can dip our toes into the infinite sea of human potential and sample the miraculous. Though the plan is to stay upright, if we get a little wet in the process, so be it. Just remember to look up.

Faith is what keeps us afloat.

2

Faith and Belief Are Not the Same

If I believe in God I have faith in God, right? Maybe. Maybe not. It has taken me a long time to realize that faith and belief are not the same, and in some cases are diametrically opposed. I wish I had known this sooner. Confusion between these essential ideas created nearly insurmountable crises of faith in my life just when I needed faith most. Searching frantically for faith, I instead pulled out an entire wardrobe of beliefs. *Surely this will fit! Surely that!* But nothing fit. And nothing matched. My beliefs, however deep, broad, educated, flexible, magical and divine, did not suit the crushing occasion. As the experience continued and only got worse, I felt terrified, naked, vulnerable, unfit, and unloved by a God I had served well. On top of everything else, I was hurled headlong into an identity crisis.

Who am I if not my beliefs?

If you've been through a terrible crisis in your life, I'm betting this has happened to you, and you are still trying to figure it out. It took me years. I think more people abandon God out of a crushing sense of having been abandoned by God first than for any other reason. But were you really abandoned by God? Or were you abandoned by your own beliefs? When faith is on the line, belief will almost always let you down. Let me explain why.

Belief is a product of the mind. A victim mind is already disadvantaged, but even a healthy, enabled mind runs into trouble. The enabled mind may say, *"God is faithful. He will: answer my prayers; cure my child; land the plane safely; reconcile my marriage; replenish my wealth. God is just and will set things right."* The enabled mind says that if we hold our beliefs strongly enough, God will listen and favor us. If we only believe! Believe in what, though? Believe in our own version of an indefinable Being who transcends us and all created things? Our beliefs are mostly narrow and rooted in culture and upbringing. Sometimes our most closely held beliefs are in direct conflict with everything else we know to be true.

If we decide or are told that our persecution is God's idea, or worse, his divine will, then how do we reconcile that deity with the God of love and benevolence? (This is so much easier when it's happening to someone else. Really. Intellectual abstraction is no substitute for direct experience.) It can be argued that we only arrive at the intersection of faith and belief when we experience a life-threatening trauma ourselves. Once we do, we may be forced to change our beliefs or go crazy. We cannot stay mentally fit as exiles of our own minds. Changing our minds means changing at least some aspect of our beliefs. Beliefs shift because beliefs are modeled on personal and/or communal experience. And a belief, just because it has been handed down to us, is not necessarily true even when we think it is. Or more clearly, it is not necessarily the *only* truth.

Belief is a product of the mind, but faith is not. Faith is a product of the spirit. The mind interferes in the process of faith more than it contributes to it. To have faith in the worst of times will no doubt require us to silence, or at least quiet the mind. Faith is what happens when our beliefs run aground. The spirit can be buoyed by our beliefs, but can also be brought down by them when they prove inadequate, as they most certainly will at some point in the journey. Even the beliefs humans have held most closely have come and gone over the course of a lifetime or a millennium. Think of Galileo.

We can believe an abstract truth, but as a result of our human limitations, we can never really know. And even our individual experiences with the same truth can collide. In time, as new spiritual and cultural information is revealed, former so-called truths can be revealed as arbitrary, false or irrelevant; i.e., slavery, polygamy, gender and race inequality, and previously sanctioned abuses by social, political and religious authorities. Beliefs come and go, but real faith is not so fickle. Real faith is not a statement of beliefs, but a state of being. It is living life midair, standing commando on a tightrope fifty stories up with no preconception of the outcome. It is trusting beyond all reason and evidence that you have not been abandoned.

Since faith is conceptual until it is put into play, it is best achieved through commitment. To commit to faith is not the same as committing to a set of beliefs. In the throes of crisis it is impossible to know what the unknowable God and/or universe is really asking of us. But in the void of knowing, we may ask, *"Is it God at all who asks this of me? Or circumstance?"* The answer of faith: *It doesn't matter.* You don't know now and you may never know. To not know in the context of faith is to remain humble and teachable. To toss away the conflicting and unusable beliefs of the mind is to be free of human chatter and hubris and a step closer to the divine. Where faith does not fill in the cracks, fear will. Faith is an attitude of acceptance of not knowing.

Knowing does not create faith. Unknowing does.

The next time you find yourself in spiritual crisis, my advice—attach no value to it, positive or negative. Release your beliefs for the time being, and do not labor at bringing them into congruity with the crisis. The crisis is likely here to teach you something that *you do not know*. Listen to it; experience its lessons. Have faith that whatever is happening to you now will be neither lost nor forgotten, but witnessed and acknowledged in the fullness of its truth.

With time and maturity, all that bears light will be made clear.

3

What It Means to Be Truly Awake

I remember many decades ago when I first heard about the now ubiquitous *Onion Theory*, how much sense it made. For those who are not familiar with it, it's as obvious as this—the self is layered like an onion. The truest part lies deep in the center wrapped in layer upon layer of experience, attachment, and distortion. At the beginning of the process, our public persona is as rough as the outer peel. To get to the center, to uncover the image and likeness of God, well, start peeling. And as with an actual onion, expect to experience plenty of tears, overexposure, and raw sensitivities that, up to this point, you may have spent a lifetime or two concealing.

Many physicians use the onion analogy to explain the healing process, as do mental health professionals and spiritual gurus. It is as apt a metaphor as we are likely to find for the journey inward. In order to find total wellbeing, we have to be willing to engage in a reverse process—the process of undoing all the negative things we have been doing, as well as the negative things that have been done to us. This is the process of waking up and becoming conscious. It is not for the faint of heart.

Although inarguably we all derive from the same Source, each life's journey is as unique as our physical DNA (and some would add spiritual DNA), so of course the process of awakening is equally unique. Even if I am experiencing the same illness as another person, I am most likely not experiencing it in the same way or for the same reasons. Even the consequences of that illness will not be the same. This is not only because we are sloughing off different layers of the onion (mine layer #3 perhaps; yours #8), but also because one person's layers cannot be compared to another's. Each layer of each onion is composed of different experiences, relationships, and belief systems (true or false) through which we process it all. This is why, on a spiritual level, judgment of others is a meaningless waste of time. What may look to be one person's ill fate or even bad behavior, may actually be his awakening—the crucial clearing of another layer of the onion. Likewise, what may look to be an awakening may be yet another, deeper journey into self-deceit.

How to tell the difference?

We can tell the difference between someone's awakening (including our own) and someone's continued, deepening hibernation, by that person's willingness to seek and effect change. It's that simple. The fruit is in the action. Real awakening involves the willingness not just to look within, but to take action; i.e., to bring ourselves into congruity with Truth, whatever that involves.

An example: Let's say you have a spouse whose chronic behavior is borderline abusive. (To simplify the pronouns I'll make that spouse a male, but obviously females also engage in this behavior.) One day you suddenly get through to him. On this one day you are able to shake him up enough to get his attention and declare the truth about how this unfair behavior affects you. And let's say this time he's really listening, so in that moment everything you say to him makes complete sense. A breakthrough! He swears that behavior is over, and you believe him. You are filled with hope.

The first time your spouse commits to this behavioral reform, you may be satisfied, but with each subsequent abusive experience, you will no doubt become more and more suspicious of his claims, because nothing changes. Although he clearly acknowledges his abusive behavior, he is in effect seeking no real truth whatsoever and therefore, changing nothing within or without. Instead of bringing himself into congruity with what he knows to be true, he chooses to remain imprisoned by the familiar discomfort and distortion that created his abusive behavior in the first place. Your husband (wife, son, daughter, parent, or self) may have indeed seen a momentary light, been blinded by it, and even wanted or tried to respond. But then came the moment of choice. Awaken and face the (sometimes blinding) light? Or remain in familiar darkness? There is always a choice. Rather than face the consequences of abusive actions and the tedious chore of acknowledging and reversing them, most people burrow even more deeply into the slumber of unconsciousness.

An awake person knows that the power to change him or herself (and therefore, the world), is the real miracle, if not the entire purpose of our material existence. It is not enough to simply notice something within us or outside of us and do nothing. Each of us is mightily empowered to effect personal and universal change every day of our lives. This opportunity more than anything else is what distinguishes us from other living things. The power to acknowledge, transform and transcend. To change. It is what we are called upon to do for our own sake and the sake of everyone else, because we are all one thing.

To awaken means to acknowledge our spiritual nature, to observe our behavior, and to bring ourselves into alignment with the Truth.

This is a process involving many awarenesses, conversions, and painful confrontations. Hard work for sure, but in the end, nothing could be more valuable or worthwhile. By doing our life's work, we are making the best use of this very brief period of empowered sentient existence to advance the consciousness of ourselves and consequently, of all humankind.

4

The Anatomy of a Miracle

I have a fairly resilient friend who's been through tough times. Her motto, borrowed from Winston Churchill is, "When you're going through hell, keep on going." Last week I asked her how things were, and she said, "All things considered, pretty darn good, but I know it won't last. Sooner or later it will all fall apart." I asked her why she thought that. "Just the way the world works," she said with a shrug.

But is it really the way the world works? Or is it possible that what we perceive as inevitable breakdowns are really caused by our failure to sustain higher thought? After all, if we expect things to deteriorate, they probably will. It makes sense that a negative expectation would set us up for failure or at least contribute to the process. Mystics and spiritual masters tell us that elements of the concrete world are first formed by substance of the Mind. In less esoteric terms that means—thought precedes action. The collective Mind is said to be infinite and unlimited. Any personal limitations are those we've probably placed on ourselves or allowed others to place on us in the form of inherited, unchallenged belief systems.

Spiritually speaking, I don't believe in limitations, which doesn't mean I don't experience any. But I realize that the limitations I do experience derive mostly from fear, unbelief, or the unforgiving boundaries of the physical world. On the whole, I'm an optimist of the supernatural sort. I've witnessed a miracle or two in my life, including the significant healings of loved ones, just-in-time money, and broader global movements like the collapse of Communism and peace in Northern Ireland. Did any of these perceived miracles contradict the laws of physics? Probably not, but they didn't occur in the absence of prayer or intention either.

Skeptics may counter (and I may agree) that in the case of medical miracles, the body has been known to muster utterly natural resources to heal itself in spite of great odds. It does happen. And money has surely been known to show up sooner or later in the pockets of intelligent, hard working people. That's how the economy is supposed to work. Of global shifts in power, one could argue that systems like Communism collapsed of their own weight decades before their final public gasp.

So if these are natural occurrences, what exactly constitutes a miracle?

Miracles spring from higher consciousness. There are plenty of gurus who preach the power of intention, and that's certainly the predecessor of any conscious act. First, we have to bring the problem and the desired result into our awareness. Maybe the sustained articulation of clear intention—to heal, to gather wealth, or even to destroy embedded social systems (especially when it's done collectively)—is enough to make it happen, if not immediately, then over time. After all, if I have a strong intention

Miracles spring from higher consciousness.

to overcome an obstacle and follow it with deliberate action, who says I can't do it? And if I do, is it a miracle or just a case of mind over matter?

Maybe mind over matter is the miracle.

Human minds are famously undisciplined. Harnessing our minds takes hard work and patience. Anyone who's ever tried to meditate knows this is true. (I have unintentionally planned entire dinner parties while trying to meditate.) The conquest of an undisciplined mind—that is, the intense and sustained focus of our inner lens on a goal of any kind—is the first and most essential step in an act of conscious creation. Consciousness is the creative force of the universe. Harnessing that force is our opportunity to partner with our Creator to produce the kind of abundant, compassionate (some would say miraculous) environment we all crave.

Not that it's easy.

At this point in evolution, unconscious creation is the norm. Unconscious creation is the product of undisciplined minds, and this type of creation is powerful, too, but in a profoundly negative way. Through unconscious creation, the mind creates situations through default. Addictions and other bad habits are given form by the constant repetition of desire and indulgence. Phobias are thought patterns created by fear. The subconscious and unconscious personal and collective mind is generally ruled by undisciplined thoughts. Repetition of these thoughts on a communal or global basis gives them form, also known as Elementals. Entire wars are caused by these—just think of the many thousands, even millions of people waking up with hatred for people they've never even met. By awakening to this hidden reality, by accepting responsibility for our individual thoughts, fears, and desires, we learn to face these enemies, reduce them, and ultimately eradicate them from within. When we reduce and eradicate them from within, it benefits not only us, but everyone in our sphere.

In other words, the entire world.

When we learn to replace negative thoughts with healthy, beneficial thoughts, we strengthen our minds and improve our lives. When we nurture beneficial elementals, we increase our ability to summon what spiritual masters called the super-substance of the higher Mind to conjure a higher world. A world that, from down here, would look pretty darn miraculous.

In one of the Christian gospels, Peter the Apostle is invited to walk with Jesus on the Sea of Galilee. He obeys, amazed at his ability to walk on water. *"Look at me!"* Reveling in his higher divine nature, he is joyful, buoyant. Then he looks down, and with his lower mind thinks, *"This is impossible! I'm defying the laws of nature."*

In that moment, he sinks.

We, too, are called to do great things, things which may even appear to be impossible. How do we prepare ourselves? First it is useful to clean house—throw out all the nasty dynamics, destructive relationships, negative patterns of thought and behavior, addictions, and sloppy living that restrict us. We have to rein in our thoughts, stop the loop of negative thinking that plays unconsciously and repeatedly in our heads. We do this through prayer, meditation, affirmations, and the will to awaken. We find a path supported by like-minded souls, eager to learn. We find a teacher, and we listen. We forget what we think we know, and summon the humility to learn what we don't. We open our minds to the possibility that all things are truly possible.

In the process, we find ourselves walking through the portal of expanded consciousness allowing the limitations to fall away, one by one, until we experience the frontier of the higher Mind where true freedom dwells. The only things we have to remember on the journey are to keep focused and follow the lighted path. Look up, not down.

And believe.

5

We're Only Human. Or Are We?

A couple of days before Christmas, a Jewish friend of ours dropped by for a visit. Slightly overwhelmed by all our paraphernalia—the tree, the ornaments, the cards, the gifts, the wrapping paper, the manger—he said, wide-eyed, "Wow! This is...amazing!"

Shrugging, my husband said, "Well, you guys have Hanukkah. We have Christmas."

"Is that what you think?" our friend said. "That Hanukkah is the Jewish Christmas?" He leaned in meaningfully. "Well, it isn't. Hanukkah is about *miracles*."

Taken aback, my husband said, "So you think Christmas *isn't* about miracles?"

On it went in a playful manner until I, mentally exhausted and anxious to see the finale of *Homeland,* sent everybody packing. Just what the world needs, I thought, another argument about religion. The things we don't understand about our own religions would fill a cosmic library, never mind other people's religions. Just the skeletal dogma alone, not to mention the infinite layers of cultural nuance.

But it got me thinking.

The next day as I ran in the park with my dog, Spirit, I wondered what Christmas (or for that matter, Hanukkah) really meant once the religious and cultural elements were stripped away, or at least neutralized. After all, doesn't every religion claim miracles? Aren't miracles the very basis of religion—supernatural proof that we aren't godforsaken?

But as an author of Visionary Fiction, for me at least, miracles are more than religious magic tricks. They are transcendent events ingrained in the human psyche, endemic to the stories we have told ourselves and recorded since the dawn of time and consciousness. Distant truths we hold sacred and deep, often defying language. *Ineffable.* Haven't we always known we were more than flesh and blood? *Isn't there more to this world than meets the eye?*

Even for the most confirmed of us, however, belief in the miraculous remains abstract and untested. Only in terrifying moments of illness or emergent death is its latent essence teased from our subconscious into broad daylight—a flicker of hope that ignites the kindling of possibility. *Maybe I can be healed. Maybe I will survive. Maybe peace is possible!* Maybe—*just maybe*—we really are supernatural creatures in spite of the gravity that grounds us.

"Simply click the heels of your ruby shoes, Dorothy. The power was always within you."

Of course, when cornered most of us don't believe we can simply click our heels, or at least not without reservation. It's easier not to believe. Not believing is a way of protecting ourselves against the odds. After all, miracles are scarce. If not, they would be reliable, quantifiable events that we humans would soon take for granted. We understand miracles to be extraordinary favors meted out by the discerning hand of a supernatural power from (name the religion). Miracles are few and far between. So if your neighbor is granted a miracle, you're probably out of luck. Right?

Not if you understand Christmas.

Before Christmas, we, through our Jewish forebears, reached outside ourselves to a distant, omnipotent God for help and liberation. God spoke to us through burning bushes, separated seas, manna sprinkled from heaven, and fuel that burned in our lamps for eight days straight. We cried out to him in anguish and desperation, and in response, he showed us his favor, granting miracles at great cost from a far away kingdom.

Christmas, on the other hand, is the story of many miracles accessible to all. It's the story of God made man. Of divinity awakened in the sleeping giant of humanity.

Christmas is not just about the birth of an exceptional man. And it is obviously not about trees and ornaments and stockings and gifts. It's about the re-imagination of humanity. It's about the incarnation, recognition, and realization of God within us. It represents the Divine element of our heritage fully-developed in an equally human Christ, a man who arrived in humility, led a life of humility, and expired by means of unsurpassable humility. Why? To redefine power. To dismiss the ego in favor of compassion. To introduce us to the angels of our higher nature. To flip the switch of infinite possibility within our minds and hearts.

Christmas is about the re-imagination of humanity.

To create abundance.

Before returning to the Father, he said of his many miracles, *"These things and more will you do in my name."*

If only we understood his gift enough to believe it. If only we believed it enough to open it.

The next time someone tells you, "You're only human," tell them not so fast. Tell them we are all equipped with the light that descended upon the Earth in an inexplicable event that produced a kind, loving, humble man who stood apart from the tribe. A light promised, not only in the Hebrew Bible, but in religions and myths that preceded those beliefs by millennia. An indefinable gift with unending potential that we are always learning to open a little bit more. It grows as our awareness grows. No one is without it. It lives among us still.

So are we human? Yes.

And so much more.

6

Lucky Enough to Die Like Dad

I f you were lucky enough to be born into the social circumstances of my father, you would be lucky enough, as the Irish say. If you were lucky enough to lead his length of 89 years, all the better, though it was not without sorrow. But if you were lucky enough to die the way my father died, or even to witness his death, your luck would runneth over. Like me, you would no doubt be left to process the miraculous nature of those events for years to come. So although I have not yet grasped it fully, I will share it anyway with hope that you will see the treasure within and claim its possibility for your own.

A bit about his life. My father and mother (who predeceased him by ten years) had eight children, one of whom died in his late twenties. My brother's tragic death cracked the shell of our imagined immortality. My parents, heartbroken, soldiered on, but were lucky enough to enjoy years of abundance with their ensuing brood of eighteen grandchildren. My mother's sudden death twenty years later widened the crack, leaving my father bereft, ambushed by grief.

A few years later, as rarely occurs, a light glimmered through that crack. An old friendship of my father's grew into an endearing companionship that endured until his death. So he was lucky enough to find love twice. His companion, Eileen, had twelve children of her own. Including our remaining seven, Eileen and Dad's list of social opportunities was long and varied. They were busier than any of their children. His life and hers burst at the seams with love, activity and joy.

My father was a religious man in the traditional sense. He followed rules, yes, but he also nurtured a deeply-felt faith and love of God. Before his last hospitalizations, he attended daily Mass, often serving as Lector or Eucharistic Minister. His faith was largely uncomplicated; he believed what he'd been taught. Although he was a well-educated MIT engineer, he nevertheless received spiritual teachings as articles of faith, not reason. He never wondered about his heavenly reward; he expected it. Which is not to say he was anxious for it; he was not. A year before his death, in order to buy himself some time, he opted for a mitral valve repair in spite of its lengthy and difficult convalescence.

The night before his death my siblings and I were called to his side rather suddenly. He had only been hospitalized a few days for what seemed an exercise in caution. When the doctors asked him why he was there, he replied, "That's what I came here to find out!" In other words, nothing evident. A slew of tests confirmed that no cardiac or neurological event had taken place. He alone sensed what was coming.

That last night he seized the opportunity to tell us individually how much he loved us and that he would continue to pray for us when he was gone. We thought he was being a bit dramatic—after all, he seemed fine. He asked us to call a string of absent and unsuspecting family members to whom he issued specific, coherent messages. He was on no medication and had crystal clarity. When his dear friend, Father Chris Isinta, anointed him, Dad participated consciously. He recited the *Act of Contrition*. Then to our great surprise, he sang a hymn into his oxygen mask and surrendered to his God.

But God didn't take him in that moment, and this confused him. "I'm ready to go!" he said. "I'm already there."

"Where," we asked him. "Where are you?"

"Paradise."

"And who are you?"

"God."

We gasped. What did he mean? Only now do I realize that God was speaking and acting through him, that he had already claimed the aspect of his nature that was divine. He was not about to surrender it and return to this broken world.

Back and forth from human to divine he moved like a pendulum, straddling the space between. The messages slipped between divine reverence and comical human impatience. "I'm ready to go," he said at one point. "Get the management! I'm supposed to be out of here by now. Nothing happens on time in this hospital!"

He clenched the sidebars of the hospital bed, squirming vertically before resting, and then repeated the action—more like a birth than a death. Alternately he struggled to a sitting position, visibly shaken that he had not yet shed his physical form. Watching this expanded my understanding of the palpability of other realms and how seamless and transparent the other side can be. How it is we who create the illusion of separation, and how easily that separation falls away when our eyes are opened, the scales removed. How could I ever question the literal reality of a paradise that my own father, having witnessed, craved so desperately he would not take no for an answer?

Early the following morning he died. One of my brothers visited the patient whose room Dad had shared that last night, apologizing for the disruption. The roommate, a Marine just back from Afghanistan, said no apology was necessary. He said that he'd talked to Dad in our absence, and they'd discussed their mutual military experiences—Dad was a World War II Navy veteran. He told Dad that times were tough for him and he felt like giving up. Dad said, "Marines never give up." He told the Marine that it wasn't his time to die, and encouraged him to live the full course of his life. The Marine told my brother that after witnessing the love and warmth of the preceding evening, he was a changed man. My father showed him the fruits of faith and persistence, his final legacy.

To those of you who have never had the gift of witnessing a man literally try to climb out of his body to receive his heavenly reward, I promise you would never forget it. It happened. I pray that one day I'm lucky enough to experience that kind of death myself. And I wish it for you.

May the road rise up to meet you, Dad, as the Irish also say. And may we all be lucky enough.

7

A Fool for Love

*L*ove is patient; love is kind; love is not envious. Love does not brag;
it is not puffed up. It is not rude; it is not self-serving; it is not easily
angered or resentful. It is not glad about injustice, but rejoices in
the truth. It bears all things; believes all things; hopes all things; endures
all things." – St. Paul to the Corinthians

What wedding guest has heard this reading and not wondered who
could possibly live up to its staggering expectation? Anyone would
agree it's impossible. Yet we include it in our ceremonies and as guests,
we listen quizzically (and perhaps with guilt), because we know
somewhere therein lies an attainable truth that we just can't grasp.
But what? Perhaps St. Paul's definition better describes parental love
than romantic love? Not likely. After all, can any parent or for that
matter, child, sibling, friend or lover, *bear all things; endure all things;
be eternally patient and kind*? No. In fact, given the long and tedious
list of our intrinsic human imperfections, St. Paul's description of

Love appears to be a futile ideal that mocks our sincerest efforts. Yet it was certainly not intended to mock. It was intended to instruct.

A lot of time and human experience has unfolded since St. Paul wrote those inspirational yet confounding words. Have we learned anything since then? In the course of those millennia, we have mostly accepted historical concepts of Love, so our collective idea of it has only marginally evolved. The concept of God's Love or '*Agape*' has been revealed, but even that Love is defined as the unconditional Love of God for humanity—something that arises from one source (albeit divine) and is shared with another. But what is Love apart from the dynamic of source and recipient, human or divine? What is the substance itself?

Although Love (as we humans have thought of it) is the source of a slew of emotions, it doesn't really qualify as an emotion. It inspires emotion, though it is not an emotion. Love is not a euphoric feeling of attachment, even though we are certainly attached to each other through Love. Neither is Love the passion or flood of endorphins that sustains romantic love or even the powerful early bonding between mother and newborn. In spite of our love-saturated pop culture, Love has nothing to do with desire, need, or hormones. We do not 'produce' Love or generate it in another. We all want it, and in a godly sense certainly deserve it, yet none of us is capable of fully manifesting it to another. Love stands outside of us and within us at the same time. It is as profound a paradox as our existence. We are saturated in it, yet tragically, parcel it out selfishly and sparingly (ignorantly) within discrete groups, consciously or unconsciously withholding it from others.

As if it were ours to give.

When we consider Love outside-the-box of emotion, our view is radically different. Freed from the confinement of convention or even the grander idealistic definition of St. Paul, Love rises to fill,

Love stands
outside of us
and within us
at the
same time.

surround, and animate the multiverse of created matter. I believe it will one day be revealed as a force of nature more profound and powerful than any of the identified four fundamental physical forces, including electromagnetism, weak/strong-nuclear force/s, or gravity. But since it isn't identified as a physical force (yet), we don't see it or understand its magnitude or availability. We mistake it for a poetic abstraction, instead of the governing ether of our higher nature. Understanding Love in the universal sense—not as something we 'feel' but as something we 'are'—has so far been the province of mystics and spiritual visionaries. But I have a hunch we've arrived at a point of evolution where that's about to change.

When we understand the nature of Love deeply, we see it in our very atomic structure and the atomic structure of all that surrounds us. When we understand Love like that, we see it as the basic component of life, a kind of spiritual/energetic stem cell. In other words the 'God Particle'—the elusive Unified Field. We are so close to it that we can't observe it without climbing a ladder to a higher perch of awareness. But we are getting there. As we learn to understand and use the substance of Love in this new way, so shall we receive it in the way St. Paul describes. Once we learn to harness its forces (or allow it to harness ours), all good things will become possible in quantum, not sequential fashion, because Love, unlike the other fundamental forces, has no duality. It is only good.

There are many who believe that a world filled with this degree of peace, love and harmony (our true nature) will exist only following an Armageddon-like event that will destroy humanity in the physical realm. But I'm not among them. I believe that the choice is always ours to awaken to higher truths here and now, and in the face of conflict, choose our weapons from the arsenal of Love. Only then will we know its strength.

Call me a fool.

8

The Good Thing About Bad Times

Yesterday was a good day in the middle of a good month in what's turning into a pretty good year. You know how it is— moments melt into hours, into days, months and years. And as good years tend to go, it's a blur. *What day is it!* What's more, I've had few distractions and fewer demands, so nothing has slowed me down from a busy and productive schedule doing the things I love. This contrasts greatly to other years I've experienced, years of mentally fatiguing and physically demanding caretaking, as well as tedious medical issues of my own. There were entire years that I was unable to gather the intellectual or creative resources to compose a coherent grocery list, never mind a publishable thesis.

2008 was such a year.

At the start of 2008, my husband and I knew we were going to move. Our children no longer lived at home, and we'd grown weary of the high finance and hard labor it took to maintain the house and grounds that had been our family home for almost 20 years. We began to prepare ourselves mentally. Where would we go? How would we live? Townhouse or single family? Waterfront or mountaintop? Fortunate to have choices (as long as the house sold), still it was daunting. Either way, the next twelve months of our lives would revolve around sorting through the substantial and sentimental artifacts of our lives, and moving on.

Or so we thought.

Although we somehow did pull off the move that year, life intervened in such a way that the move was the least of our work. While trying to plan our future, we endured the acute critical illness of one of our children, followed by unexpected surgery of my own. The same day our house went on the market, we received an offer that was rescinded two weeks later because the buyer, along with nearly everyone else at Lehman Brothers, was fired when the market crashed. A second buyer stepped in on the condition we get rid of a half-buried oil tank. Ironically, the tank sprung a leak from the preliminary pressure test, requiring an indeterminate period of soil remediation as we all wondered if the seepage had contaminated the ground water. There's much more, but you get the point. Suffice it to say, we were ecstatic to see 2008 drag its catastrophic butt offstage and into the drama archives.

Seven years later, I have a slightly different perspective.

The thing about 2008 and years like it, is that even now I remember nearly every detail. I remember how I felt (scared). I remember what songs played relentlessly on the radio (Leonia Lewis' *Bleeding Love*; Jordin Sparks' *No Air*). I can still recall the anxiety that shot up my chest without warning like rockets of sulfuric acid. I remember swallowing the fear so it wouldn't converge with the fear of my husband and children, consuming us. I remember the fear, but

I also remember the kindness of friends, the skill of doctors, the generosity of nurses, and the penetrating sense of gratitude I felt at the resolution of each crisis. How I fell to my knees and wept.

In 2008 I meditated faithfully to release the stress that clung to my core gravity like rusty nails. Stress that begged the questions: Would my child survive? (He did.) Would I? And on a lesser scale, would our house sell in the middle of a global economic crisis? What if it didn't? *What if it did?* Would I overcome the compounding grief of leaving the home that had sheltered my young family? Would we find another home that made us as happy? Our stress quotient was stratospheric.

Because of that, 2008 was a bookmark year.

I remember the chapters that preceded 2008 and those that followed. I remember everything that occurred with a clarity that informs how I process nearly everything that has happened to me since. I ask myself, is it as bad as 2008? No? Okay, then I can handle it in my sleep. And that makes me realize that if it were not for the bad days, life might slip away unnoticed—a rapid succession of innocuous moments flowing into a refreshing but undifferentiated pool of time.

Kind of like now.

So am I asking for trouble? No way. Would I invite suffering upon myself? God, no. I strive to hold every moment in a chalice, sacred, and still they slip away. But one thing I've learned is that trouble likely appears for a reason, and it pays to understand its purpose. Suffering grabs time by the ankles and slows it down, forcing us to stop, stand our ground, look around and take stock. *Who are we? Why are we here?* Through our loss and near-losses, we come to acknowledge the shocking miracle of our own existence.

Suffering is the spiritual fuel that transforms us from the inside out, consuming our egos in the process.

Gurus of every nature encourage us to live life in the moment, it's true. And I've done more than one essay on that subject. But there are times when living in the moment isn't enough unless we expand the moment to include its context. There are times we have to draw back, remove the telephoto and snap on the panoramic lens to evaluate the bigger picture. (*Ah, so that's where I am!*) Only then will the tiny incremental moments have meaning. We can seize the moment, seize the day, or seize the life we've been given. When we pull back and allow it in, the suffering and the joy, we seize it all.

And through it, we are changed.

Wise wo/men say we can't do any of this well without faith, but what does that mean exactly? For me, the measure of mature faith is the ability to become comfortable with *not* knowing if the house will sell and when; if the market will recover and when; who will survive and who won't. (Spoiler alert: no one does.) The measure of mature faith is the understanding that the adventure we're all living is larger and more complex than even the most enlightened of us could ever imagine, never mind control.

Suffering is the spiritual fuel that transforms us from the inside out, consuming our egos in the process, if we allow it. (Allow it.) Then one day, out of nowhere, a castle appears in the rearview mirror on a high peak at the edge of a vast wilderness. From one of its many balconies one can view the panoramic sweep of a hard-earned life, well-lived. A conscious life of compassion and purpose. And suddenly it all makes sense. We turn and retrace our steps, remembering as we go. This is where I learned humility. Forgiveness. Compassion. Empathy.

This is where I discovered my humanity.

9

Are You 'Exactly Where You Are Meant to Be'?

There is a prayer that endlessly travels the web, containing the line, *"May you trust that you are exactly where you are meant to be."* Depending on your life, situation, or the day you're having when you run across this line, it may lift your spirits or crush them. Personally, I feel that the idea expressed in this line is mostly empty, deceiving, and in some cases even harmful. Why? Because what we say, especially in prayer, matters deeply. Thoughts are the seeds of words; words the seeds of action.

For those of us who are digging out of a negative situation over which we are finally exerting some control, the line *"You are exactly where you are meant to be"* might be true and validate our efforts. In other words, *"I am where I am meant to be because I am doing what it takes to climb out of the hole I (may or may not have) dug."* In such a case, I have risen above victim consciousness and assumed responsibility for my life. I am accountable.

But am I exactly where I am meant to be if I'm begging or stealing from others because I'm miserably addicted to the prescription drugs that once saved me from pain? No, I am not. In that case, where I'm meant to be is rehab. Am I exactly where I'm meant to be if I'm hungry and homeless? No. In that case, if I'm unable to work or can't find a job, I am meant to be receptive to the compassion of my friends and family, or really, anyone who's willing to help. No one is meant to live without shelter or in a chronic state of fear and anxiety. We are meant to seek solutions, and with personal accountability and the compassion of others, we are meant to lift ourselves out of misery and hopelessness. Misery and hopelessness are nobody's intended fate. If you are miserable and hopeless, you are not where you are meant to be.

The idea that at any given point in our lives we are exactly where we are meant to be assumes that (if things are good) we are blessed by a loving God, or (if things are bad) we deserve whatever cruelty is being served up. As a sweeping statement, that line is no more than another rung in a system that lets the rest of us off the hook. When we see someone suffering, we can dismiss it because *"they are exactly where they are meant to be."* In that case we can hang out and wait for someone else, maybe God, to perform the miracle that will rescue them. Worst of all, if this prayer is passed onto us in our despair, we are left in that despair because the only conclusion we can draw is that, if this is true, we are meaningless to God and worse, God and the ones through whom God works are masochists who have left us to suffer.

Are any of us 'meant to be' in prison, ICU, or rehab? Not unless we or our circumstances have put ourselves there and those places are the wombs of our rebirth. Otherwise, no. We 'are meant to be' personally accountable, highly compassionate, joyful children of our Creator. This notion that we are other than that depicts us as victims riding a never-ending karmic wheel. We may as well just stay put and see where it takes us. (I'll spare you the suspense—it takes us down.) The karmic wheel accounts for cause and effect (some say over lifetimes). Stop the cause and you stop the effect. Personal accountability, not only for ourselves but in compassion for those who need us, puts us on a different course. Personal accountability makes us worthy instruments of God. When we are personally accountable ourselves, we can do God's work.

You are exactly where you are meant to be if you are filled with peace, acceptance, compassion, and love for your fellow humans. If you are in pain that cannot be resolved and for which you have reached no acceptance—if you are lonely, unsettled, depressed, anxious, enraged, filled with hate or resentment—you are not where you are meant to be. Pain is not a companion. It's a reset button.

Get help.

10

God, Spiritual Evolution, and Internet Porn

O ver the holidays, a friend expressed grave concern to me about the devolution of humanity as aided and abetted by the Internet. "How can we get anywhere when Internet violence and pornography sabotage us at every turn?" he said. "It's so bad, and we stand to lose God in the middle of it."

This was not the first of such conversations I've had with people in the 40+ age group, people who have raised or are still raising teenagers. It's a big social issue and a losing argument in many households as kids (and adults) find ways around moral codes and digital firewalls. It's easy to find whatever you want, good or bad. The Internet has unlocked the basement door and thrown away the key.

For the sake of clarity, I'm defining porn loosely here as the general tendency to degrade ourselves and others, not just physically or sexually, but also socially and intellectually. In other words, porn in this context is anything that appeals to our lower nature, including violence of thought, word, deed or animation. And while I find all of the above as offensive as anyone, I'm surprisingly less pessimistic about it. I don't think it will destroy the planet or arrest the evolution of our collective consciousness. I don't think it signals the end of God or decency. In fact, I think the exposure of our moral underbelly is essential to the future of humankind, and possibly the only way out of the global sinkhole we've created.

Here's why:

The Internet on its own is not essentially good or bad. It's a tool, a searchlight directed at us—our attic, our living space and our basement. And as it turns out, the basement is filthy, swimming in debris and crying out to be cleaned. What shows up on the Internet is merely a reflection of what's already present in our individual and collective consciousness. It's nothing new. Maybe it's 10 percent high-order transcendent thought and 90 percent polluted filth, but that might be optimistic. Choose your own numbers. Whatever it is, it is, and we're all getting a good look at what really attracts our attention. The monsters of our lower nature have driven us mad for millennia with pride, greed, bias, rage, addiction, enslavement, rape, entitlement, loathing, and whatever other deficiencies you can name. They have run rampant in the dark since the dawn of consciousness, chained occasionally to the stone walls of our psychic dungeons during brief periods of enlightenment, but never for long.

Now they are free.

They are free to roam larger than life, 3D, LED, LCD, and whatever else technology dreams up next. Now the monsters have dimension and light. We have no choice but to acknowledge and address that, *"Yes, we do think these things, imagine these things, entertain these things that have the power to degrade and wound us."* And they have certainly wounded us. But wounds cannot be treated and healed until they've been lanced and exposed. The Internet exposes them.

Almost a century ago, the great visionary, Teilhard de Chardin, identified a membrane of thought that wraps around the Earth. He called it the 'noosphere' (no-o-sphere). The noosphere, he claimed, indiscriminately contained whatever thoughts we humans have contributed to it over time, conscious, subconscious, and collectively unconscious. There's no taking them back. It is the witness of our existence, proving that our thoughts have mattered much more than we ever knew. Before the Internet, we could mask them in darkness; hide them in basements. In hiding them from others as well as ourselves, they were often not clear or obvious until they did damage. Before Twitter, Facebook, and all the rest, only a master psychic or disastrous slip of the tongue could indict us for a lewd thought, biased opinion, or hateful barb. But now our ideas, opinions and attitudes toward each other are as transparent as our words and deeds. As Teilhard also predicted, the noosphere is waking up.

In his book, *The Phenomenon of Man*, written in the 1930's, but published in 1955, years after his death, de Chardin wrote:

"A glow ripples outward from the first spark of conscious reflection. The point of ignition grows larger. The fire spreads in ever widening circles till finally the whole planet is covered with incandescence. Only one interpretation, only one name can be found worthy of this grand phenomenon. Much more coherent and just as extensive as any preceding layer, it is really a new layer, the 'thinking layer', which, since its germination at the end of the Tertiary period, has spread over and above the world of plants and animals. In other words, outside and above the biosphere there is the noosphere."

He believed that as the noosphere spread over the surface of our globe, Idea would meet Idea, and the result would be "an organized web of thought, a noetic system operating under high tension, a piece of evolutionary machinery capable of generating high psychosocial energy."

In other words, the Internet.

Looking at the Internet this way does not remove our responsibility to protect our higher nature from the pull of gravity. But it does allow us to see what really belies our human pain. It's a mess down there. And just maybe that energetic/spiritual mess is also affecting our mental and physical health and the health of our planet. Blinded by the light of the Internet, maybe now we'll be able to own up to it. Maybe in acknowledging the real status quo, we'll be able to reinforce the positive aspects of our humanity. In reinforcing the positive aspects of our humanity, maybe we'll see the critical importance of learning (and teaching) profound inner spiritual and moral discipline.

And in the end, maybe that was always the way up the basement stairs.

Now our
ideas, opinions
and attitudes
toward each other
are as
transparent
as our
words and deeds.

11

The Best Marital Advice

At a wedding I attended recently, the minister told the couple, "My advice to you is not to try to change each other. It's a waste of time. You are who you are, and the same is true of your partner. Respect that. Remember who you fell in love with in the first place."

I've heard that marital advice from the altar more than once, and I cringe every time. Not that I advocate bullying an introvert into becoming a party clown, for instance; I don't. It wouldn't work anyway. Certain aspects of our personalities are hardwired. So yes, accept the fundamentals. Respect your partner's need to socialize periodically, or conversely, to recharge his or her batteries in the garden or on the golf course. But there's a lot more leeway for change than those homilies suggest. My advice to married couples is, "Challenge each other to grow. Challenge each other to evolve into the people you were meant to be."

Growth is an essential dynamic of life, and growth requires change.

When I was in college I had a wonderful friend named John. He was a self-improvement guru way ahead of his time. He meditated, practiced yoga and led a pretty Zen life. Not that he didn't have to work at it; he did. Peace, I've discovered, requires more work than conflict, at least on the front end. I called him once (back in the landline-only days), and there was so much friction that I didn't recognize his voice. "Is this John?" I asked.

His answer, "Not yet, but I'm working on it."

That remark stuck with me in a primal way. It's my go-to whenever I think I can't travel any further down the road to self-improvement. I never forget it or its powerful implication that from the beginning of our lives to the end, we are works-in-progress. We must change, individually and collectively, not just to thrive but to survive at all. In our early years we are mere spiritual stem cells of who we are meant to be. But how do we fulfill that destiny? How do we get there? Not with rigidity, that's for sure. Not by insisting, "I am who I am and stop trying to change me." There is only one road that will get us there, and that road requires courage, flexibility and openness to the many challenges along the way.

That road is awareness.

Awareness, or consciousness, though present in each of us in differing degrees, doesn't magically show up or evolve. Some people never expand their awareness, spending their entire lives surrounded by the mirrored walls of their own fixed opinions. Awareness isn't a passive process; it doesn't come knocking on your door. It must be pursued, cultivated and earned. Awareness is the only escape from ego. It's our connection to the divine. We don't cultivate awareness for our own sake, although we will certainly benefit individually. We do it for each other, for our spouses, families, friends, associates, and really, everyone. We cultivate awareness for humankind.

A healthy marriage helps us rise above our individuality to a higher good for a higher purpose. It helps us to cultivate awareness. By fully committing to someone else, we learn the limitations of self-defense and self-protection as a lifestyle. Awareness within a committed relationship moves us closer to empathy and compassion and acceptance of issues we may have previously viewed as strange or foreign. The plan is that we will eventually be able to extend those lessons beyond our marriage into our families and communities, resetting our internal GPS's from local to global. The growth of one affects the growth of another, and another, on and on until nothing is foreign or strange, and we have busily created the Kingdom of God on Earth one person at a time.

At this point in evolution, we humans are still a scorekeeping species. We seek the win, the one-upmanship, the higher rung on the ladder. We are competitive and exclusive. But relationships are adverse to scorekeeping. In marriage, when you win, you lose. The question we should ask ourselves is not, "Did I win that last argument?" but, "Did that argument bring my marriage closer to union or closer to separation, and what was my contribution to it?" This kind of thinking requires awareness.

Although awareness is the road, it's not the destination. The destination is unity.

Unity is critical not only to marriage, but to family, community, country and planet. Unity is the goal and purpose of our existence. Every relationship is meant to teach us how to work for a common good instead of our own self-involved pursuits. Every relationship is meant to teach us the benefits of unity and wholeness over separation and fragmentation. Employing the governing principal of Unity v Separation, committed relationships can teach us to put

A
healthy marriage
helps us
rise above our
individuality to a
higher good
for a
higher purpose.

our egos aside. Ask yourself, "Will the thought I'm entertaining—the word, the action or decision I'm about to make—bring this marriage closer together or further apart? Will it prop us up or pull us down?" Awareness is the only tool in the cosmic belt that allows us to answer these questions with any integrity.

Everything we do to improve ourselves and our relationships—listening, caregiving, forgiving, supporting, sacrificing and celebrating—contributes to our personal and global evolution. Gaining personal awareness changes how we relate to each other personally, locally, and globally. It changes how we relate to the Earth that feeds us, and to the divine Source that sustains our spirit. There is nothing that isn't changed by the conscious growth, however small, of a single individual.

Life is a journey, and if we emerge at the other end exactly as we arrived, we have accomplished nothing. So couples, for the sake of us all—please change! And remember to support each other in the process.

12

Do Not Love Your Neighbor as Yourself

At least not yet.

Loving our neighbors as ourselves is one of the overarching spiritual laws of our time. It is an irreducible commandment, intended to remind us that we are bound to each other by compassion. It seems obvious that such a way of life would be the panacea for all social maladies, including perhaps the deterioration of civilization itself. If we are keeping our neighbors on equal par with ourselves and our families, then we are bound to build utopian communities, right?

Only if we love ourselves. And there's plenty of evidence out there that many of us don't have a clue how to do that.

I have a neighbor I'll call Alice, who is anxious, overwrought, and succumbing to increasingly poor health, including a complex of diseases. Alice has a spiritual mentor who recently told her to put life on hold and take time for herself. "It's critical to your health that you learn to put yourself first," her mentor had advised. When Alice confided this to me, she said, "I know she's right. I put everyone ahead of myself. Tomorrow I'm going to show myself some love. I'm going to do some shopping, get my nails and hair done, see a movie and go out to dinner." She was elated that someone had given her permission to indulge, permission she really didn't need since overindulgence was at the heart of Alice's issues in the first place.

Although there's really nothing morally wrong with the way Alice decided to interpret her mentor's advice that day, I was a little speechless. I know Alice's mentor well, and I also know that the last thing she intended was that Alice would take the day to shop, pamper, and generally consume. What she'd intended was for Alice to get to know her spiritual self on a deeper level. She'd wanted Alice to disconnect from superficial influences in order to reconnect to her higher nature. She was saying that Alice's spirit was starved, in desperate need of nourishment. But instead of nourishing her emaciated spirit, Alice feasted on material goods and mental distractions.

Alice isn't the only one who interprets self-love as self-indulgence. We've all been there. This is exactly what the billboards tell us to do. Addictions abound in a self-loathing cycle of overindulgence followed by regret, followed by deep-seated denial, and repeat. Is this how we wish to treat our neighbor? Probably not. Yet, we cannot treat our neighbor well if we mistreat ourselves. We cannot love our neighbor if we do not love ourselves. To love ourselves is not to gorge on the empty calories of consumer distraction, creating sloth and depression. Real self-love calls for a steady diet of spiritual practice capable of rebuilding our divine connection.

The exquisite Maya Angelou said, "I do not trust people who don't love themselves and yet tell me, 'I love you.' There is an African saying which is: *Be careful when a naked person offers you a shirt.*"

To love ourselves in a manner that will strengthen our spirits requires discipline, not indulgence; silence, not noisy distraction; emptiness, not consumption. To begin, pick a time and stick with it, starting with just five minutes a day. During this time:

1   Banish all devices that connect you to the outside world.

2   Refrain from food, drink, chatter, any form of stimulation or material goods.

3   Choose a private area.

4   Sit quietly and concentrate on your breath.

5   Invite the Divine Presence into your space.

6   Place yourself in that Presence with anticipation.

7   Gently turn away all mental thoughts as they intrude.

8   Feel love and allow that love to redefine your intrinsic value.

9   Increase this special time in increments of five minutes (as you are ready) until you are able to feed your spirit this feast for 20 minutes at a time with less and less distraction.

10   See yourself as part of a living whole that is bound by love to all creatures.

Loving yourself now, you are free to love your neighbor with the same depth and compassion. In time, it will change you, your neighbor, and the world.

13

How to Get the Most Out of Time

T ime is tricky. For one thing, there's never enough. Though physicists see it as a flexible commodity, no one's signing up for shuttles into time warps or wormholes anytime soon. It will be a while before we can board a train for the Inauguration of King Henry VIII, for example, or attend a space concert in the 31st century. For now, the rules are rigid. Every moment, every day, every lifetime is packaged with a beginning, a middle, and an end in that order. No exceptions, though durations vary.

Time is vexing because we who dwell within it are timeless creatures. Our true nature is eternal. If you ever doubted this, consider that we are born utterly unaware of time; as children we fight it relentlessly; as adolescents we rail against it; and even as adults, we struggle to conform. Some of us never figure it out. This is because time is a foreign element that imposes limits on an otherwise limitless nature. The mind wanders in other dimensions, even as our bodies

Time is vexing because we who dwell within it are timeless creatures.

are rooted to this one. It can take us on a trip to Paris while we're strapped to a dentist chair enduring root canal. Conversely, it can replay an old argument a hundred times in the middle of a spectacular ballet.

We're not always where we say we are.

Time is a worthy opponent. And the thing about opponents is—the tougher they are, the more they teach us.

We are born; we live; we die. Time provides beginnings and ends, sequence and order. It provides frame and form. It strengthens us through the discipline of cause and effect. It challenges us to consider our options, but urges us to act now. Seize the moment or it will disappear. As we age, most of us learn to look through the windshield instead of the rearview mirror. We learn not to dawdle in the past or pine for the future. Time is one of the few things that can force our minds into the here and now, though it isn't always successful at it. By applying consequences, it teaches us to loosen our grip on the past so we can create a future out of the awareness we cultivate in the present.

Like most opponents, time at its best is an effective agent of change and transformation. Ironically, the transformation time creates, stands outside of time. That's because transformation creates awareness, and awareness doesn't die.

Time delivers awareness through timeless events like birth and death. The births of our children open portals of awareness so surreal, you may not even understand what's happening or how to articulate it. What's happening is the expansion of time. Moments feel like hours and hours like moments in one breathtaking experience that changes everything. After 24 hours of labor followed by the birth of my first son, my obstetrician said, "I don't care how long you've been awake; you won't be able to sleep. No one is." The births of my sons taught me that time doesn't always have the last word. When enough awareness is applied, time stops, opening slowly like a lotus, revealing its deepest secret layers.

My father's recent death expanded my awareness even further. Interestingly, as he grew older and less able, I found myself subconsciously devaluing his remaining time. After all, what could he do with it? He could barely read a book or follow a conversation; what insights could he share? There was evidence that his mind was becoming as arthritic as his body. But that isn't how time works. Time doesn't care how old or young we are. Its secrets are democratic and universal. We have the same access to the miracles of time on our last day as we do on the first, maybe more. I say more because through the passage of time, we have more likely increased our bounty of awareness.

On my dad's last day, the transformative power of the present moment—the Eternal Now—was as available to him as it was on the day he stood on the brink of manhood. It was at work transforming his infinite potential until his very last breath. My siblings and I could see that something was happening with him, but what? It was obvious and mysterious at once. Just when we thought his awareness was buried beneath the rubble of a lifetime, it danced on stage in a top hat and cane in a spotlight that illuminated eternity, not just to him, but to every one of us through him.

An earlier essay of mine elaborates further on my dad's death, but suffice it to say here that what he gave us at the end was not the time-decayed leftovers of a once relevant life, a life that had run out of time. What he gave us in the end was the most valuable part of himself—his eternal awareness. Through him, we experienced the true present, the Eternal Now. We couldn't miss it. And in your time, if you remain open, you can experience it too. The awareness of death and dying and the world beyond time that he shared with us in his final moments serves as inspiration to us every day. It was his real legacy. And it came to us ripened, full-bodied, and inspired, exactly as it was supposed to and when—in his final moments.

Our lives are shaped by our mortality. Knowing from the beginning that we are going to die brings value to the currency of time. But it also deceives us into thinking that as we go forward, one moment is less valuable than the next. That youth has more value than age. It deceives us into thinking that we are not important unless we are shielded by years, or even decades of potential. It deceives us into thinking that the last breath is less valuable than the first. Yet it is far more valuable, because potential increases and compounds with years. And in the end, if we have used time wisely and learned to transcend its limits—if we have opened our hearts to awareness and cultivated compassion among us—we will open up to the Godhead like the portals of time, in layers of unimaginable joy and ecstasy.

Every moment matters.

14

Five Steps to Getting Your Life Off the Ground

W e can all appreciate the tailwinds in our lives, the ones that carry us unobstructed to our intended destinations. A good tailwind delivers big rewards with little effort. If we experience it early enough in life, we may mistake it for routine, or at least our routine. We may even wonder why others, caught in the headwinds, are unable to move ahead as quickly, or at all.

But no matter how lucky or grand our circumstance, sooner or later our personal headwinds will prevail. It's inevitable and even necessary. Why? Because headwinds are critical to personal development. They don't just slow us down and force us to focus, they generate lift. They carry us up. Aeronautically, headwinds assist in takeoff as well as landing. In life, they are the bearers of challenges and confrontations meant to hone us into the people we are meant to be. Whether they hone us or defeat us depends on our navigational skills.

I spent the first 30 years or so of my life in an exhilarating tailwind. Everything was, I thought, as it should be—exciting, combustible, hilariously funny, and assisted by an intoxicating rush of momentum. Looking back, I see there was some headwind even then, but the tailwind was so substantial that I barely noticed.

After college and some grad school on the East Coast, I moved to Mountain View, California. Call it destiny or dumb luck, my advertising career was launched in Silicon Valley just as the electronic giants were taking off. I rode that tailwind to quick success, never really understanding the altitude I'd hit or how rarified the air I was breathing. For me, it was just the way things were.

A few years in, I hit some significant headwind, not to mention crosswinds that generated enough force to knock me out of nearly every preconceived notion I had about life. First, I relocated to Chicago for my husband's job, and started an advertising agency with a partner. My business thrived just as my young marriage fell apart. I adjusted to a new home in a new city while starting a new business with a partner I'd worked with only briefly. As intimidating as that may sound, I was still in the throes of a substantial tailwind. On the wings of the emerging, crippling emotional illness of my husband and a crumbling marriage, I was forced to slow down enough to look my life in the eye and consider a change in course.

Looking back, I see that it was the unwelcome headwinds that forced me to develop and improve my navigational skills, my inner GPS. Critical skills I would desperately need later in the face of much greater storms. How far would I have gone, I wonder, without these skills, never really looking too far up or too deeply within to understand that life is, or at least should be, fueled by compassion, not money or the illusion of success. I was lucky to learn these lessons early. It would be fair to say that I might have avoided that initial headwind by being more astute in the first place. But I know

now that it wasn't the headwinds at all I should have avoided. It was the turbulence.

And turbulence, I've learned, comes largely from within.

My life had a plan, and the only flaw was that I thought I knew what it was. The navigational skills I developed in my first headwind taught me to awaken and take responsibility for my life. It taught me patience, resilience, and the kind of faith that got me through future cataclysmic events, like the death of my young brother and the critical illness of my child.

Your life has a plan too. But in order to get to it, you have to release your resistance to the offending situation, in other words, your headwind. You have to learn to accept it so it can lift you up and reveal its insights. Persistently countering resistance (about anything) from bosses, coworkers, family members, or a significant event—creates turbulence. Tailwinds can't carry a static rigid object where it refuses to go. All it will do is rock you and your grief back and forth interminably until you release the rage, disappointment, frustration, or disbelief that prevents you from rising above your shattered expectations. If your headwind wasn't issued by an illness to begin with, you are in danger of becoming ill anyway from the inflammatory nature of your acidic emotions.

Releasing resistance and stagnation is generally not an automatic response, except in transcendent beings. It's a learned process. If you are inside a significant headwind right now and turbulence is intolerable, I offer you a daily visualization to speed the process along, lifting you up and out.

1   Remember that your headwind is here to teach you something important. If it weren't important, you would not be experiencing so much resistance.

2   Go 'soft body'—release the physical tension. Lie down in a comfortable place and feel the tension from head to toe. Moving slowly from the top of your head to the bottom of your feet, slowly release it.

3   Next, imagine yourself suspended vertically in a river of deep blue energy. Your entire body is surrounded by it. Your hair drifts upward. Your arms float. You are completely supported by the water.

4   Take stock of your body and note the location of any blockage—the area in which your turbulence is stored. Is it your head? Lungs? Liver? Lower back? Spend an extra few minutes visualizing and releasing it from that spot until you genuinely feel your entire body and everything in it, float.

5   Now visualize yourself not as a solid mass, but as a transparent element in the river. Picture the crystal blue energy flowing through you, back to front, without obstacles, stagnation, or resistance. The river and you are one. You are exchanging energy freely. Remain with this visualization for at least five minutes, aiming for a goal of 15-20.

Whenever we encounter a genuine life obstacle, the only way to put it behind us is to move through it. Defending our previous position, nursing the wound, railing against God and the universe for allowing it to happen in the first place, may feel good at first, but eventually it compounds the pain. At some point, if we choose to go forward, we have to get back up. By eradicating or even reducing our inner turbulence, we invite the headwind to raise us up to a new horizon.

Whenever we encounter a genuine life obstacle, the only way to put it behind us is to move through it.

15

Spiritual Lessons from the Plant World

Long before I met him, my husband was lugging a hardy split-leaf philodendron state to state, house to house. Some forty years from the day he first acquired it, it lives with us still. We call it the monster, because no matter how much we ignore it, it refuses to die, and worse, seems to nearly double its foliage every year. Since we've recently downsized, there's little room in our home for such grandiosity. At the earliest sign of spring, the monster is dragged outdoors to the patio where Mother Nature nurtures it at her whim. Since it unfailingly thrives, we reluctantly drag it back in at first frost. It had grown so much by the end of last summer that my husband decided to cut it in half. Instead of tossing the offshoot into the river at my suggestion, he secretly potted it and presented it to me as a gift.

"You must be kidding," I said. "We barely have room for the mother."

"Let's just put it in the bedroom and see what happens," he said. "Maybe it won't grow."

He is such an enabler.

Conducting a quick tour of the bedroom, anyone could see there was no room for a plant with this much ambition. Alas, he found a dark corner behind the door of the master bath next to the tub. "This will do until spring," he said, plopping it down. I watched helplessly, hoping the monster clone would hate it there, wither and die.

But no.

Less than a week later, leaf after giant, brand new, spring-green leaf shot three feet up and unfurled in a mocking fashion. As upset as I was, I couldn't help but admire the core strength and bodacious vitality of this invader—just the self-confidence alone! Soon I would be climbing around it to get into the tub. As the weeks wore on, I began to feel a certain weird intimacy with it that messed with my conscience. I could feel myself mentally backtracking on my scheme to kill it with malign neglect. Guilt unfurled in the pit of my stomach with each new leaf, and three weeks in, I broke down and watered it.

The following week during a blizzard, I opened the slats of the plantation shutters behind the tub to create enough light to apply my makeup. The slats were generally left closed for privacy reasons, but I figured on such a dark, blustery day, no one was likely to stop by. I left them open. Later on when I reentered the room, I could see that every new leaf of the monster clone had traveled intentionally toward the window, bending dramatically to reach the light between the slats. I was in awe. This thing was alive in a way I hadn't considered. It seemed to possess not the passive sort of awareness we tend to ascribe to the plant kingdom, but an active, opportunistic intelligence. I realized then that on the most fundamental level my needs and the needs of this goliath were the same.

We both sought light.

This plant's stubborn determination to stop at nothing to express itself has had a surprising effect on me. In a way, it's helped me to expand my own horizons. Gradually backing down from my former bias, I was able to appreciate so much about my cellmate, like its wildly verdant vitality against the backdrop of winter desolation. Its survival instinct staggered me.

Over the years (and especially this last year) I've learned that the more we evolve into our authentic selves, the greater our connection to the animal, plant and mineral kingdoms that surround us. Attuning ourselves to higher purpose, we resonate with the elements of nature that have been placed in our care. (Everything has been placed in our care.) The more we evolve, the more we understand that all living things are imbued with the breath of creation. This unwanted stepchild of a plant exchanged breath with me—my carbon dioxide for its oxygen. Ultimately, I was at its mercy as much as it was at mine.

What did I learn from my interloper? Five things I can think of offhand:

1   Be yourself unashamedly.

2   Be patient with your caretakers.

3   Thrive where you're planted.

4   Always move into the light.

5   Sometimes you have to come face-to-face in a tight spot with a big obstacle before you figure out its lesson.

It's nearly spring now, time to drag it back out to the patio. I wonder if I will.

16

Does Suffering Bring Us Closer to God?

I know it's a popular theory that the means to God is through suffering, but to be honest, I'm not a proponent. In fact, I'm not a believer in suffering as a means to anything, really, except pain. When my son was critically ill, some well-meaning people would say, "We're so much closer to God when we're suffering," and I would think, "Are you crazy?" The truth is, I never felt more distant. And neither did my son. I watched helplessly as his faith dwindled and crashed out of a sense of sheer divine abandonment. *"My God, my God, why have you forsaken us?"* Godly people, we had expected a sense of overwhelming peace and protection that would see us through the worst. It never came. And whereas canned theology says, "God is always with you," that's far too simple and obtuse a concept when you are starved for consolation.

No, I am not a believer in suffering as a means to God. But because so many spiritual teachings promote that theory, I have investigated it as thoroughly as a person in a single lifetime can. What I have found is that suffering works well in the lives of people who have been running in the wrong direction, in which case pain can be a valuable reset button. In those cases, pain has the power to stop the momentum and turn a person around in the right direction, the direction of hope, light, and awareness. But suffering can also enter a conscious life of right action and abiding goodness, and in this case it has the power to diminish or even extinguish that faith. And although the suffering may be endured and endured well, it can be many years before that faith is repackaged and returned in a coherent or recognizable form. This is what St. John of the Cross called *The Dark Night of the Soul.*

It is said in the sacred traditions that suffering has the power to empty us of the false self. That in great suffering, we are brought before God emotionally naked and that only in that nakedness can we be re-dressed and strengthened. As Thomas Merton wrote, *"We are all a body of broken bones in the process of being recast."* And although I understand this perspective well, I nevertheless maintain that Love, not suffering, is our best teacher. That God is Love, and suffering has less to do with God than with our broken-down world. That in fact, God abhors suffering as much as we do, and empowers us to end it.

Perhaps I feel this way about suffering because mine is not, nor has it ever been, a punishing faith. I have been born into and sustained a spirituality of great joy and abundance, a bounty which I have appreciated greatly and made a conscious effort to pay forward. Still, in my life and in the lives of good people I have known, great suffering has been unavoidable. So here's what I've learned.

I've learned that in the midst of the terrible suffering of a loved one, it is sometimes impossible to find God, because it is here that God enters us in extreme and unfamiliar ways. While we are desperately searching everywhere for divine nurturing and care, it is instead we who have been empowered by God to provide that care for another. In my case, it was my son. While he and I were looking everywhere for the divine support we craved, we forgot to look at each other. How we were surviving. How we have continued to survive. How? How did that happen?

I believe now that it happened because I had been duly empowered to attend to the myriad emergencies—to hold him when he cried; to endure his pain and despair; to feed him; to make him laugh; to watch him fall apart; to put him back together again; and again; and again. Somehow I had been mysteriously empowered to do nearly impossible things. Things I thought I would never be able to do. Things I certainly hoped would never be required of me. And in allowing me to do these things for him with gratitude, he returned the favor.

The concept of God using us this directly in times of extreme suffering is a foreign one because we are nervous about the idea of being consumed by God. Of *becoming* God. After all, who are we? This is often a case of false humility—false because when the self is no longer present or active, neither is pride. When the self is gone and pride is absent, there is only God. The One. The Source. While it is easy to understand the concept of 'doing God's work', in extreme cases I believe it goes further than we dare to look. Deeper. It is no longer a 'doing' but a 'becoming'.

You have to know what to look for.

If right now you are in an extreme situation, searching everywhere for God, and God is nowhere to be found, look at yourself. Not just 'within' but 'at'. Look at your actions. The expanding magnitude of your love. Your ability to be present in the face of great pain. To look it in the eye and stay put. Look at your ability to endure and persist and continue to put everything aside but this—your ability

I've learned that in the midst of the terrible suffering of a loved one, it is sometimes impossible to find God, because it is here that God enters us in extreme and unfamiliar ways.

to love. Or if you are the sick one—your ability to respond to that love. To receive it.

Here you will find God.

It may be that in your suffering, your familiar faith has been disabled because it wasn't massive enough to accommodate the approaching transformation—the spiritual alchemy of an ever-present, ever-loving God who, for a time, in order to take care of you, became you.

17

Why You Might Not Be Free

This year, instead of anticipating a July 4th filled with barbecues and fireworks, I find myself pondering the real meaning of freedom—how some are free and others are not. How there are people even in this free country with no freedom at all. Freedom is not one thing. It is an ideal that manifests in many forms. Like everything else in our world, it has three components— physical, mental/emotional, and spiritual.

The physical aspect of freedom involves, among other things, our surroundings. Where we live matters. For some, freedom features wide open spaces, abundant nature, lots of elbow room—a farm, perhaps. For others, that version of freedom is a prison of isolation and backbreaking work. For city people, freedom is the ability to press an elevator button and stroll outside into the melée, the diverse culture of theater, restaurants and music. In an ideal world, we would all have the freedom to live where we choose. But what if, through marriage, economics, old age, illness, or even war we found ourselves in circumstances that oppose our fundamental picture of freedom? Could we survive? Could we thrive?

That's where the mental/emotional component kicks in. We've all heard the adage, 'bloom where you're planted'. Not always easy. My personal story is a case in point. When I met my husband, he lived on a horse farm in Virginia; I in a Chicago townhouse. After years of back and forth, my husband's dream prevailed. We moved to the farm. The reason his prevailed is that I was more flexible and adaptable. Why? Because my idea of freedom was more mental than physical.

Even so, it wasn't easy to go from the rich social culture of Chicago to the silence and isolation of a Virginia farm. It took me two years to grow roots in that soil. I had to get used to the rural culture, which at the time contained biases I didn't share. I had to forgive, banish judgment, and seek the profound goodness that I knew was in there somewhere. In time, I grew to love the people and their ethic of hard work. Seven years later when we moved to the Northeast, I was extremely sad to leave. Even now, twenty years later, I still dream of the undulating 35 mile view of pasture, horses, and four-board fencing from our bedroom window. It was an honor to have lived there.

I viewed my return to the Northeast, however, as another opportunity. I adapted more quickly this time, because I was near my family, the boys were in school (easier to meet people), and in spite of the population and traffic density, there was an explosion of culture I was apparently starved for. I jumped right in.

Not everyone can adapt that quickly, I know, because I see it all around me. I see it in people who, in spite of opportunity, never considered leaving the area of their origin. Sometimes staying close to home is a clear choice, but sometimes it's a product of fear. Fear of stepping out of the comfort zone. Even in a philosophically free world, fear can handcuff any of us in a moment. Just ask the ill and the elderly, the physically and mentally impaired, or those who are frustrated by lack of finance or opportunity. Frustration is hard to put aside; it can kill motivation and forward movement. Frustration is just one of many mile-high mental/emotional fences that can keep us from our intended lives.

As a young prisoner, Dr. Viktor Frankl (1905-1997) did a phenomenal job of investigating the ultimate frustration and devastation of physical and mental confinement in WWII concentration camps. The extreme examples of survival (or not), of flexibility and adaptability (or despair) that he describes, provide the key to human motivation. Why did some persist and others desist? Frankl didn't see it as luck so much as an element of personality and worldview. For some, life was worth living under any circumstance, and for others, it simply wasn't. (Read *Man's Search for Meaning*—a life-changing book!)

Frankl would probably agree with Thomas Merton (1915-1968), a (mostly) cloistered monk, that the answer to the question of true survival is based on the third type of freedom—the spiritual sort (by which I do not mean religious). Merton led a licentious, intellectual and cosmopolitan life prior to his calling. By all accounts, he should have panicked and reversed direction when he arrived at the cloistered cell of the monastery in Kentucky. His new life was an imprisonment of isolation, labor, and enforced silence. In a cell!

Instead, he called it, "These four walls of my new freedom."

For Merton, incarceration wasn't the physical cloistered life he'd chosen, but the one he'd led accidentally—the one bound by destructive habits and personal attachments. In his confinement he was able to free himself and the planet through a constant stream of contemplative prayer and sacrifice. He was free to remove himself from all that was temporal, temporary and false, and replace it with all that was eternal and true.

I read an article in the paper many years ago in which the author decided to try meditation in a 'why not?' mood. After a week he said he couldn't believe he'd waited so long. Within his quiet seeking he was unexpectedly ambushed by love. Meditation and contemplative prayer are the spiritual means for people of any religion or culture to directly experience true freedom from confinement or hardship. It contains no words, no ideas, no concepts or belief systems, no barriers to truth. Through these higher forms of prayer, we enter 'the inner room', the Tabernacle where we are confronted with the infinite bodiless, mindless freedom of our common Source. It has to be experienced to be believed.

In the end, the only true freedom is the spiritual form, because once attained, it can never be taken away without our consent. Physical and mental freedoms are conditional, but spiritual freedom is not. It is the great equalizer, endowed on anyone with the awareness to ask.

In the end,
the only true freedom
is the spiritual form,
because once attained,
it can **never** be
taken away
without our consent.

18

Is Your Story Dragging You Around?

You don't have to be a writer to have a story. Everyone has one. The accumulation of our experience adds up to the mysterious calculus of who we are and who we are becoming. This depends largely on the dynamic between us and our experiences, especially the traumatic ones that seriously challenge our emotional and spiritual growth. Have we responded positively to these traumas? Or reacted from a negative instinctual place? Are we still reacting? Do we over-identify with that earlier pain and suffering? Have we become it? Do we lead every conversation with our wounds, or do we identify with the exhilaration of having overcome the obstacles that once pinned us to the past?

I've had more than one significant trauma of my own, so as both a spiritual mentor and teacher of writing, I've thought a lot about how I knocked down those obstacles and got moving again. For me, the only thing more devastating than a tragic experience would be to allow it to dominate the rest of my life.

Where to start?

Visualize. In the initial stages it helps to see the trauma as a tractor that drags us everywhere it goes, which is everywhere our random and afflicted minds let it wander. In this stage, the trauma informs the Mind and the Mind informs the (submissive) spirit. The body is often an innocent bystander assaulted by the catastrophic hit of stress hormones that comes with being perennially stuck in a rigid negative state anchored to the past. If you've ever been there, you know how hopeless it feels. But if you visualize your tractor well enough and understand the dynamic of authority, you can change that.

Seize Authority Over Your Thoughts. That means identify, recognize and refuse the thoughts that chain you to your tractor. Though this is admittedly difficult at first, with time, commitment, affirmations, and positive reinforcement you can eventually picture yourself catching up. Once you've caught up to your tractor, picture yourself running alongside it. Keeping pace. Are you moving with it, or is it moving with you? It doesn't matter. In this stage you are still attached, but your forces are equal. You are gaining authority. You can't stop now.

Own Your Spiritual Power. Since we are all made of the same divine matter, you are only a spiritual lightweight if you allow yourself to be. Don't allow it. With continued time, patience, resolve, discipline, and spiritual practice, you can gain enough strength to stop your tractor in its tracks. Visualize it parked in a fixed space. Walk around it. Kick the tires. Unplug it from its fuel source. Disable it. When you no longer share the fixed mental space of your tractor, you are in charge. At this stage, it's a reference point, not a vehicle. It can't take you anywhere.

Lose the Victimhood. In other words, step ahead of your tractor and don't look back. This is the stage at which your Spirit informs your (now submissive) mind. When the Spirit begins to inform the mind instead of the reverse, the information flow between all aspects of your being gains quantity and quality. You have momentum. You are no longer locked in a linear progression, but floating freely in the infinite holographic universe with countless positive, powerful points of contact. You are where you are meant to be.

Forgive. I realize it's difficult, but we literally can't move forward without forgiveness. It shackles us to the past. We don't have to shake hands with our trauma or our abuser, but we do have to forgive God and the universe for allowing it to happen in the first place. This takes humility. Humility is a grace that will open you to understand what it is you do not know about your trauma, and may never know. Without humility, only the deceptive linear pattern experienced by the five senses and a traumatized mind is apparent. This gets you nowhere. By leaving victimhood behind, you will regain dimension. As an enabled spirit with power over the past, you will gracefully arrive at gratitude which will drop you off at peace.

Forgiveness, gratitude and peace are catalysts of transformation and enlightenment that you did not possess before the trauma took place, at least not to this degree. In the end you will see that the tractor has not taken you backwards, but dragged you headlong into a new world, if you allow it. (Allow it.) It has dragged you into a world that features hope and possibility even in the face of tragedy. You have stared your trauma down and walked away.

Grant Yourself Permission to Live. You will access the trauma periodically, of course. But when you do, you will be an observer not a participant. The trauma will no longer contain you. You will contain it. You will contain the trauma minus the mental involvement and chaotic energy that left you deeply injured and exposed in such a way that it became your only story. Now it's one story. One of many. Now it's a story that taught you compassion in the face of loss; forgiveness in the face of attack; love in the face of hatred; freedom in the face of isolation. This is your passport to a joyful and creative life.

Be Free.

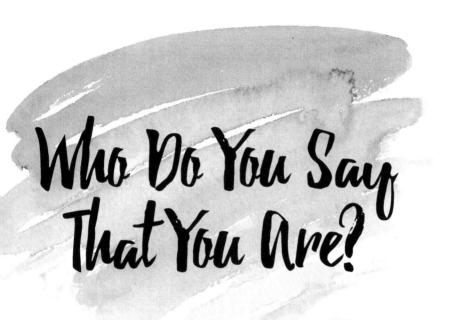

19

Who Do You Say That You Are?

Other than the significant ongoing issue of women as deacons and priests, Pope Francis is everything I ever wanted in a pope. He is Christ in the temple overthrowing the money changers and upsetting the power cabal of the corporate religion. He is, so far at least, the man of the hour rising to every occasion, pastoral and political, identifying with his flock instead of the elitist hierarchy. In light of all that, I risk sounding small-minded when I ask him to think twice before he identifies himself, or really any of us, as sinners first.

Don't get me wrong; I sin. And even before Francis said so, I knew he did too. I suppose admitting it in public is a different thing, especially for a declared holy man who has pledged himself to the highest moral code. For the rest of us, though, sinning is old hat. As a cradle Catholic I was accustomed to piously pounding my chest in mea culpa to the *Hail Holy Queen* and any number of other prayers that required it, including the *Kyrie, Eleison* during Mass. I have a collection of old, family holy cards that use language like "Lord, forgive this miserable sinner..." which my grandmother had me repeating after her when I was five years old. I continued mindlessly repeating it until I was in my thirties, when I suddenly realized there was something inherently wrong with the interior message I was sending myself.

We all sin to varying degrees and frequencies, depending on our definitions of sin, which might vary in the context of our indulgent culture. We humans are as imperfect as anything you're likely to find on this entropic 3-dimensional plane. We're a bit lazy or maybe a lot. Even the best of us gravitates toward breakdown, decay, potato chips, hot fudge sundaes, a few glasses of cabernet and the most convenient way of getting anything done, which often involves corner-cutting. And well, sinning.

But with all due respect to the spectacular new pontiff, a sinner is not who I am, or for that matter, who he is. Or anyone. At least not who we *really* are. Identifying ourselves as sinners is unhealthy, and when you think about it, has gotten us absolutely nowhere in the last few millennia or so, except into a lot of trouble. It's a bar so low we have to stoop to reach it. At best it inspires humility, as with Francis. At worst it inspires devastatingly low self-image, utter lack of self-esteem, and the kind of grossly debauched behavior that meets even the most lax definition of sin.

The great St. Catherine of Siena (1347-1380) wrote some beautiful verses in her short life. One of my favorites is quoted in the book, *A Catholic Book of Hours and other Devotions* published by Loyola Press. Referencing the Incarnation of Christ, she wrote, *"Through this union of divine nature with human nature, God was made human and humanity was made God."*

Who we
tell ourselves
we are,
matters.

Not just Christ, she says, but all of humanity was "made God". This includes you, me and Francis. This is the higher bar. This is a bar we have to climb a few ladders, stand on tiptoes, and lean forward to reach. This is a bar worth reaching.

I often think if we filed the emblem 'sinner' into the folder: *Older Paradigms of Victim Consciousness*, and opened the folder: *Children of the Most High*—we might work a little harder at cleaning up our imperfections. After all, by every account we are created in the image and likeness of God. My true identity is a child of divinity, who in partnership with that divinity (as well as with my husband) co-created two magnificent children. I truly hope that those two magnificent young men will humbly reject the destructive identity of sinner on their way to claiming the divine legacy to which they and all of us are truly destined.

So if not sinners, then who are we really? We are noble creatures endowed with a wealth of holy spiritual gifts that we are charged to develop and share generously with each other, the animal kingdom and the Earth. If we see ourselves that way, maybe we'll behave that way.

Who we tell ourselves we are, matters.

20

10 Ways to Stop Sabotaging Your Health

So you're not feeling great. Maybe you've been diagnosed with a borderline condition—cholesterol or blood pressure, fatty liver, pre-diabetes, or early signs of arthritis. You're sent home with strict instructions to take better care of yourself. You do your best. You buckle down for a while, buy a gym membership, eliminate sugar, add fiber, consume the recommended supplements. Maybe you even go vegan. Months later, your lab results still aren't in range. Soon you'll be on those pills you swore you'd never take.

How do you turn this around?

Doing everything in your power physically and nutritionally are obvious elements of healing. But there's usually more to it. The body is an incredibly intelligent, interactive biological and energetic matrix that in most cases is ready and willing to cooperate with our best efforts. But sometimes we are our own opposition. If we have bodily complaints, one reason may be that we spend too much time complaining about our bodies.

We've all recited the mantra: *"You're not thin enough. You're not tall enough. You're too busty. Too flat-chested. Too ugly. Too gangly. Too ordinary. Too pale. Too dark. Too old. Too little. Too much."*

Poor body image is an epidemic that at best sends us to the gym and diet counselor, and at worst creates disorders like depression, malnourishment, anorexia and bulimia. But these are only the obvious and conscious manifestations of the dialogue we have with our bodies. Much more occurs in our internal organs that may take decades to surface.

If you've explored holistic therapies, you're familiar with the concept of Mind/Body as an inseparable unit. If you think you're telling your body one thing and it's doing the opposite, think again. It's possible your inner subconscious track is giving your body a different set of messages. The Mind's contribution to your physical condition is significant. Ideally, the Body receives what the Mind sends, processes it, and issues a response. If you're well-tuned, happy, active and eating well, you are most likely supporting a robust immune system that will in turn support a confident, balanced, and expansive Mind. The health cycle thrives.

However, if you repeatedly transmit negative messages, they too, will take root in the body.

Decades ago, an auspicious trip to a recommended acupuncturist introduced me to a labyrinth of knowledge, both physical and emotional. Through many years, practitioners treated my body as a tightly connected system of meridians that corresponded not only to the outside world (via environmental, energetic, and dietary influences), but also to the inner world of my own thoughts and emotions. As above, so below. By exploring acupuncture and other ancient and contemporary energetic modalities (that are now mainstream), I came to understand the emotional messages I was sending, consciously or unwittingly, throughout my Mind/Body network, and where they landed.

According to Traditional Chinese Medicine (TCM), as well as other ancient therapies, every emotion has a corresponding organ. These organs help us to process the stress created by feelings we can't (or won't) shake. If we understand the connection, we can cooperate with the process and learn to resolve emotional issues. If we don't, our organs may store that stress, risking stagnation and disease.

TCM teaches that emotional repositories are distributed throughout the body. For instance, the **lungs** are said to process grief and sadness. When grief and sadness are acute, the lungs become stressed, making us vulnerable to short-term infections and chronic disease.

The **liver/gall bladder** stores unprocessed anger, frustration, rage, bitterness and resentment.

The **kidneys** store unprocessed fear and terror.

Unprocessed 'frightful sadness' is stored in the **heart**.

Unprocessed hurt, a sense of depletion, and the inability to express emotions are said to be stored in the **pericardium, brain, pituitary and reproductive organs**.

The **pancreas and spleen** store unprocessed over-thinking, worry, and low self-esteem.

The **stomach** stores unprocessed disgust and despair.

Understanding and interrupting negative emotional patterns is one of the most useful tools at our disposal for improving and maintaining health.

The **large intestine** receives unprocessed emotions of guilt, defensiveness, and the sense of being 'stuck'.

Feelings of insecurity, vulnerability and abandonment are processed and stored in the **small intestine**.

Irritation and timidity affect the **bladder**.

If we evaluate our organs in response to these associated emotions, it may reveal a pattern. Exposing a pattern may make us more willing to evaluate lingering issues in our lives, such as accumulated guilt, resentment, or lack of forgiveness. We may understand more directly the need to remove ourselves from abusive or otherwise hurtful situations. We may be more proactive in resetting career goals or leaving a frustrating, dead-end job. We may be willing to confront our addictions. Understanding and interrupting negative emotional patterns is one of the most useful tools at our disposal for improving and maintaining health.

How to stop sabotaging yourself:

1   Spend more time listening to your body and less time complaining about it.

2   Determine what your body is trying to tell you.

3   Catch yourself whenever you're tempted to undermine any aspect of your body, superficial or functional. (For example, instead of saying, *"This damn knee...hip...shoulder"*—send love to the injured joint, which has, after all, served you well up to this point.

4   Identify the areas of concern and the associated emotions.

5   Consider addressing these concerns early on through medical and complementary therapies such as acupuncture, Natural Force Healing, therapeutic massage, chiropractic, yoga, REIKI, and other energetic therapies, as well as psychological counseling.

6   Learn to meditate. Meditation gives volume to your inner voice.

7   At the end of every day, acknowledge your body, concentrating on areas of inflammation, infection, or chronic discomfort.

8   Send gratitude like a waterfall from the top of your head slowly down the neck, chest, abdomen, into your internal organs to your legs, and finally into your feet which map your body and root you to the Earth. Give your body the appreciation it deserves and visualize repair.

9   Expect wellness instead of illness.

10   Be prepared for a change in course.

21

You Can't Feed Art to a Hungry Man

These are gritty times. The economy is unstable. Racial tensions are stratospheric. Rebellion is global. Hunger abounds. The last thing we need right now is a bunch of dreamers dreaming up some new way to paint, sing, write or dance. What we need right now are soldiers of reality—pragmatists willing to roll up their sleeves and solve concrete problems in concrete ways. Right?

Well yes, but.

Last night I was flipping through a catalog brimming with colorful photos of exquisite handmade jewelry, crystal sculptures, hand-hooked rugs and original oil paintings—all stunning to behold. About halfway through, I thought—why am I even looking at these things? They're beautiful, yes, but superfluous in a world where the environment is endangered and the food is contaminated. Where refugees everywhere are fighting for their lives and disease is rampant. Who cares about a $70 crystal blue Swarovski unicorn? (It's very cute.) I wasn't even considering the gold embellished mahogany sculptures of mama and baby panda at $2,500 each. (Also adorable, but I'd have to sell a lot more books.)

But then I thought, what about the people who create these magnificent works? Skilled artisans who no doubt labor for years over a single painting or decorative rug? If nobody buys this art, they'll starve. Artists deserve to eat, too. Don't they?

I went round and round with this thought throughout the day, lugging it to the grocery store and okay, yes, to the shoe sale at the mall. I wondered, what's heavier on the scale of justice—the love of art, music, literature? *The need to create?* Or the impoverished, suffering masses in need of food and shelter? Inspiration or desperation? It drove me a little crazy, because after all, what kind of world is so pragmatic it excludes creative pursuits? What would that kind of world do to the artists?

What would it do to the rest of us?

It brought to mind a book I'd read decades ago, entitled *Power vs Force* by the late eminent scholar, David R. Hawkins, M.D., Ph.D.—a life changing book about the evolution of human consciousness. Big ideas broken into palatable bite-size pieces. In it Hawkins maps degrees of consciousness and the behaviors that correspond to each level from a baseline of bare physical survival all the way to the ecstasy of enlightenment. It accounts for how different we all are; what each of us sees and how we see it. Through Hawkins' keen lens, we understand why some civilizations prioritize war, while others prioritize opera.

According to Hawkins, the lowest level in the human experience is the consciousness of Shame. Interestingly, this corresponds with the reported consciousness of our earliest ancestors, Adam and Eve, whose universal tale was spread by word-of-mouth in many ancient cultures before it was ever written in the Bible. Adam and Eve, banished from paradise, it is told, covered their nakedness with Shame. I think we can all agree that there was little room in their lives for free verse, experimental dance, or a Mozart concerto. Hawkins characterizes Shame with Humiliation, Elimination (murder/suicide), and a Despicable 'God-view'. In other words, a state of emotional self-loathing and spiritual impoverishment. Love and forgiveness can't survive in an ecosystem of Shame.

Neither can art.

According to Hawkins, the natural course of evolution moves us from Shame to the level of Guilt, followed by Apathy. On our way up (believe it or not), we step on Fear, followed by Desire, Anger and Pride in that order, to arrive at Willingness, which is the gateway to light.

Willingness is a window, a safe landing, a place of reflection. When a person (or civilization) is Willing, s/he sheds despair and aggression to embrace possibility. *"Maybe I'm okay. Maybe you're okay. Maybe there's more to life than Shame and Humiliation, Guilt and Condemnation."* Willingness to listen to a new way of thinking and behavior is just the beginning, a portal to higher pursuits. The Renaissance was a fertile bed of Willingness—willingness to seek knowledge, to learn and grow. Willingness is characterized by Optimism, Intention, and an Inspirational 'God-view'. After Willingness, we move up the ladder to Acceptance, Reason, Love, Joy, Peace, and at the pinnacle of consciousness—Enlightenment.

But Willingness is the watershed where art becomes possible.

When we arrive at Willingness, our hunger shifts from the body and mind to the Soul. This is the moment when art in all its forms—visual, performing, musical, and literary, are cultivated. Art feeds the Soul, reminding us that there is more to life than the obvious. There is also subtlety, perception, grace and joy. Not to mention Love.

> *"Art can die. What matters is that it should have sown seeds on the earth...it must give birth to a world."* — Joan Miro

The great philosopher and psychiatrist, Carl Jung, drew parallels between art, human dignity and inspiration. Where one exists, he said, they all do. Without dignity and inspiration, we subsist on the lower levels of consciousness. Without art, without inspiration, we gorge on a toxic cocktail of Humiliation, Blame, Regret, Anxiety, Addiction, Hate and Scorn. (Now there's a hangover.) Art reflects potential. Visionary art in all its forms shines a light on the next step of the ladder, giving us something to reach for. Without it, humanity is stuck in a zero sum struggle for survival.

I'm not saying that luminescent painting, whimsical lyrics, or even a crystal blue Swarovski unicorn will feed a hungry man.

Or am I?

22

Religion Does Not Contain God

Sometimes I think we've got it backwards. We think religion—yours, mine and ours—contains God, when in fact it's the reverse. God is infinitely larger than any religion could ever be, no matter how global, dogmatic or grandiose. God is the infinite structure within which every religion is contained. Within which we ourselves are contained. If we think of religion that way, we may be more open to the many true things religion does not mention about life in general. The many things it doesn't mention about God, for that matter.

All sacred texts contain many teachings that are bound by time, culture, and the limitations of the human mind and experience. However God is not fixed in time. God is eternal. Sometimes I wonder about how difficult it is for God to reach us through the extreme limitations of the human mind, even the minds of mystics and prophets. Our human awareness, or consciousness, is

If we truly understand the infinite nature of God, we might give our Creator a little more room to breathe.

continually evolving, so it only makes sense that the prophecies of our times would be very different, and possibly even contradict, the prophecies or mandates of ancient people.

If we understand better that God contains us and our religious beliefs instead of the reverse, we might think more about how we've tried to confine God to our specific and rigid belief systems—belief systems that sometimes show themselves over time or personal experience to be conditional or even false. If we truly understand the infinite nature of God, we might give our Creator a little more room to breathe—to speak through different types of people in different cultures with different priorities. We might not set ourselves up for failure by creating literal and absolute profiles of a Creator who is, let's face it, largely unknowable to our imperfect minds. We might listen better to the ideas of others in the human family and not freeze our spiritual evolution at a temporal time and space that is fixed for all eternity. Anything fixed is human, after all, because God cannot be pinned down anywhere in the space/time continuum except by us and our perceptions, true or false. If we think of God this way, as the Infinite Unknown, we might be willing to understand that the religious ideas we have inherited or discovered, however true, are a fraction of the divine information that is continually being imparted from the spiritual domain.

When I think about the idea that God contains us fully and not the other way around, I become more humble and receptive to the ideas of others, though I am not advocating lack of discernment. But if instead of reaching for systematic dogma or defining God through rigid systems of any persuasion, we instead openly seek Truth, I think we have a better chance of actually finding God.

23

How to Manifest Your Dreams

I remember a particular New Year's Day in my mid-twenties when I was full of resolve. I was living in a Chicago suburb, where I managed a profitable business in a career I loved, owned a charming country home, and from any other perspective, held the world in the palms of my hands. No resolutions required, right?

Wrong. I was miserable. Over the previous year I'd fallen steadily into a funk that I was unable to define or escape. It just *was*. Or so I told myself. That year I made a resolution to turn my life around—to really change things. And even though there were obvious external issues at play, I began with the only person I knew would not disappoint me. Myself.

In an effort to improve my life, I joined a health club, worked out relentlessly, and adopted a spectacular Great Pyrenees puppy. I got more fit, made more money, and read more books. I advanced my skills and my career. I made more friends. On weekends, I poured myself into gardening, improving our little country acre to the best of my ability. I sought improvement everywhere and in everything I did.

By the end of that year, I was more miserable than ever.

If my life were a road trip, you could say I was driving without a view. I'd carefully scrubbed off all the gnats and sticky pieces of travel grit, and still came up with zero visibility. Why? Because with all my hard work and good intention, I'd avoided the single largest obstruction on the windshield.

At some point I would have to face my hopeless relationship.

We all do this. We make resolutions to improve our lives, to seek greater awareness, to become more compassionate beings, whatever the lofty goal. Yet we work around the elephant, not only in every room, but also splashed across the windshield of our dreams, blocking our potential. In my case, the elephant was an unhealthy relationship. For you, it may be a job, career, education, health, dysfunction in the family, difficult roommate, or an addiction you just can't (or refuse to) acknowledge or overcome. So instead, maybe you also join a health club, bump up the nutrition, and attend retreats to appease the emotional exhaustion created by the elephant you are so busy climbing over and around, you can't see straight. Here's the thing. It doesn't work.

You'll never get where you're meant to be if you can't see the way.

How to begin:

Make yourself roadworthy. If you want to make essential progress in your life's journey in the next year, the first thing you'll need is a vehicle. That vehicle is you—body, mind, and spirit. You can't get far with a banged-up car. Whatever it entails, bring yourself into balance. For me, it's good nutrition, exercise, prayer, meditation, creative work, and energetic therapies, like acupuncture and Natural Force Healing. These steps are preliminary, ongoing, and crucial. At any given point, if you're out of balance, your view will be distorted.

Define the destination. Roll out the map of your life, beginning with childhood, and identify the activities that gave you the most joy and stimulation. Prioritize them. These are the gifts and personality archetypes that drive you. If you feel no particular connection to specific activities, your mission this year is more exploratory. Sample new things. Join groups. Paint, sing, dance, hike, travel. Make mistakes. Find your compass by changing direction. Identify the path you've walked up to now, however accidental. See how it varies from the one you'd envisioned, and plan how to bridge that gap. If you've never envisioned a life path, this is the time. Create it now.

Dream big. Dreams are the unedited creations of the imagination. They represent our best selves. Don't limit them, at least for now. Place everything on that map that you can imagine would provide fulfillment. For some it will be an expansive, even a global life plan, including extensive travel. For others, it will be an inner journey of spiritual exploration. We're all standing at different points on the path, and our experiences, dreams and intentions will naturally reflect that. Once you've planned your itinerary, identify any obstructions or impasses you foresee. Address them before the journey begins. It may delay your trip a bit, but with courage, ingenuity, and perspective, most impediments can and should be overcome.

Choose your passengers wisely. Look around. Are your present companions the people you would take on a lifelong road trip? A single vacation? A night out? *None of the above?* Do they enhance your life? Advance your dreams? Offer wise counsel and faithfully nudge you in the right direction? Are they dependable? Do they bring you joy? (Do you bring them joy?) Act accordingly. If there's work to be done in this area, including counseling, do it before you get in the car.

Open the windows and put the top down. In other words, open your mind and prepare to learn. This journey is about authenticity and growth. It's about becoming who you really are. The people, places and mode of transportation you choose, via job, lifestyle, hobbies, or even recreation, are not only your chauffeurs, they're your teachers. If you choose carefully, you'll experience joy, focus, fascination, and serenity, but also the discomfort of having moved beyond the familiar. Feel that discomfort, sit with it, and learn from it. It's the bridge from your old life to the new. Trust that its invaluable importance will be understood and appreciated when you're waving to it in the rear view mirror, if not sooner.

When I look back at my younger self that year in Chicago and all the unrest that followed, I see those years as my greatest achievement. Those were the years I broke through my comfort zone and dared to dream. Those were the years I acknowledged my own worth and invested it in the future. It might have taken some waterworks to clean up that windshield, but I'll never regret it. Everything changed from that point forward. Now, most of the time the view from my windshield is crystal clear.

When it isn't, I know what to do.

You'll never get
where you're
meant to be
if you can't
see the way.

Are We Living in Biblical Times?

I hear this phrase frequently, and think—are these times inherently different? Larger than life? Miraculous? Or like the great flood, globally destructive? Whether you're religious or not, 'Biblical' evokes images of a strategic shift, the metaphorical fork in the road, times when philosophies, actions and the course of human events are a magnitude above the usual order. For doomsayers, such times predict catastrophic change. Zealots wait, not in fear, but in eager anticipation of the rising of the faithful and condemnation of the damned. Are we in the midst of that?

Or something else.

If religious conflagrations are any indication, maybe Armageddon really is at hand. Religious flashpoints are as dense and widespread as the unprecedented population of our planet. The rise of nationalism is epidemic. Nationalism contributes mightily to the

Facing ourselves in this realm of transparency for the first time in human history is as epic as the introduction of sight, sound, smell and touch.

fracas, encouraging conflict and separation over peace and unity. Contentious rhetoric, civil upset, and belligerent policies fan the flames of religious and cultural competition on an international scale. The world is a tinderbox with a nuclear match.

At their core, these issues are not unique to our times. They have always existed. At least they've existed (to varying degrees) in previous 'systems of thought'—or 'paradigms' as they are called—in human history. Paradigms, however, are 'Biblical' in importance. For one thing, they are few and far between, sometimes centuries or even millennia. Paradigms are critical to the evolutionary direction of human destiny. They are the conceptual structures that support our intellectual, emotional, and spiritual growth. Paradigm leaders include spiritual icons of all religions and philosophies who have catapulted our thinking into previously unimagined realms of thought and action. Love over hate. Peace over violence. Generosity over greed. Unity over separation.

The seeds of earlier paradigms are still within or at least among us, represented by entire groups of people, even nations, who are either resistant or have not been exposed to the next order. Sometimes this is due to insular or defensive thinking. Sometimes it's due to physical isolation, poverty, violence, or a life of abuse that has rendered them reactive to the past. People who are reactive or stuck in the past build walls, take prisoners, and reject outside communications. They cling to the familiar, even if it's destructive. They are ruled by fear.

In their day, older paradigms served great purpose, lifting humanity to higher planes of thought and behavior. Even an 'eye for an eye' was a massive improvement over the torture previously inflicted on prisoners in ancient Babylonia. As barbaric as it seems now, Hammurabi's code represented a paradigm shift in justice, allowing the law to extract from the perpetrator only what was taken from his victim. It could have been so much worse. Other paradigm shifts over time took us from victim consciousness to the awareness of individual power. Paradigm shifts have moved us from superstition to evidence-based science, from autocracy to democracy, from slavery to freedom. But what's next? If we are indeed living in 'Biblical' times, we are headed for a shift.

When a paradigm no longer serves evolution, it recedes and deteriorates from lack of energy. As it deteriorates, there are always those who will declare it the end of civilization, of humanity perhaps or the world as we know it. There are those who would rather die than accept a new order. But a paradigm whose time has come will situate itself no matter what. It has generally been quietly doing just that, for decades or longer, in the backdrop of day-to-day life. If we recognize it, we can save a lot of time and grief by helping it along. As Nietzsche said, *"That which is falling must also be pushed."* In other words, when the world is falling apart, there's a reason for it. Push. Help make room for the new.

New paradigms are seeded in the minds and hearts of visionaries— mystics, prophets, artists, and inspired leaders. They begin as possibilities, grow to probabilities, and as more people become attuned consciously or subconsciously, they become inevitabilities. When activated, new paradigms brew a powerful evolution of mind and spirit that has the ability to ignite a fire of higher thought over time even in the most reluctant. Each paradigm shift requires a brand new medium, or culture, in which to grow. The substance and structure of that culture is often so revolutionary, it cannot be predicted before its time.

Paradigm cultures differ dramatically. The culture of a paradigm shift for our times, for example, would be drastically different than the Age of Enlightenment when science made its startling debut. At that time, the printing press made information widespread and accessible to ordinary people, allowing the ideas of the new paradigm to likewise spread in unprecedented ways. The culture for our paradigm shift also involves communication, but in an exponentially more ubiquitous way. It is the ability to communicate anywhere instantaneously with almost anyone—to literally speak our minds without opening our mouths.

The culture for our new paradigm is the Internet.

To be clear, the Internet is not the paradigm; it is the medium, the soil in which the paradigm grows and is nourished. What the Internet provides on the surface is information, but what it provides from a paradigm perspective is a window into other dimensions, dimensions that were always here, but beyond our seeing. These are the dimensions of thought, where past, present, and future are indistinguishable. Where the laws of time and space are nearly irrelevant. Where everything that ever was, continues to exist simultaneously.

The new paradigm has arrived in the disguise of a business tool, but its purpose is spiritually transformative. Through it, we see what has always been true—that our thoughts have form. And power. We not only see what that means, we experience it. We see that our thoughts exist now and always; that they are witnessed and stored. We see that a single tweet can sweep the globe in seconds; that our thoughts not only have speed, but direction. We see that we cannot retract them; that we must learn to control them. In order to move on, we must hold ourselves accountable for our thoughts and their impact on others, and in so doing, understand the true power of the mind and its derivatives.

For now, we are novices—outraged when publicly convicted of something that was previously considered private. Facing ourselves in this realm of transparency for the first time in human history is as epic as the introduction of sight, sound, smell, and touch. It is a tectonic tool of intellectual, psychological, and spiritual transformation—the entire Collective Mind of humanity stripped of its fig leaf. Only through this kind of transparency can we clean ourselves up to prepare for the next step—unity. This is a paradigm culture that for the first time not only supports, but accelerates the evolutionary process. It's a shift beyond our imagining, and yet we are well in its midst. But is it 'Biblical' in proportion?

You bet.

25

How You Can Stop a War. Yes, You.

Philosophers, yogis and mystics have long studied the etheric super-substance of Mind from which thought derives. The consensus across all disciplines is that a single thought (good or bad) dwelled upon over a period of time takes form. These forms are known as Elementals, and Elementals are responsible for everything from the brief grace of a found parking spot, to the debilitation of addiction, to the enduring curse of terrorism or war. Since these elemental energetic forms are first issued by and then entertained in our conscious and unconscious minds, we can stop them and their negative effects by cultivating awareness. In stopping them (refusing to return the volley), we have the potential not only to prevent family feuds, famines, and holocausts, but in their place, create a wealth of joy, peace, and love.

There are surprisingly specific mechanics to this process. Mystics from many spiritual traditions believe that a thought exits the forehead, amplifies as it travels, and enters the intended recipient at a magnitude of exactly 7 times the energetic intensity it had at conception. This dynamic applies to positive thought forms (prayers and blessings), as well as negative thought forms (conscious curses or the unconscious transmission of fear). The surprising power of these Elementals, they say, accounts for the phenomenon of déjà vu, thinking about a person moments before they call, or developing a sudden sense of urgency about someone in distress. If you are especially 'sensitive' or 'intuitive', you are tuned-in to the mental messages that are sent your way. The more sensitive you are, the earlier you'll pick up the message. The earlier you pick up the message, the faster you can accept (or decline) its intended impact.

If all day long we are sending out (intended or unintended) negative thoughts, receiving them at a magnitude of 7, repackaging and redelivering them at another magnitude of 7, and on and on, then without even opening our mouths, we are engaged in an extremely destructive dynamic. As this continues back and forth over the course of a day, a week, or a month, it is compounding resentment, anger, and hostility that becomes harder and harder to resolve or even articulate. After all, no one is taking responsibility for the ill will. Understanding this complex dynamic makes it easy to see how negative thoughts, including anxiety, addictions, self-defeating attitudes, depression, rage, and hatred can manifest into enduring personal, communal, regional, national, and even global catastrophes without anyone accepting blame or understanding their participation.

But the good news is that since it emanates from us, we also have the power to stop it.

By recognizing our participation in a destructive dynamic, we not only have the power to neutralize it, but to convert it to a blessing. Though we can't stop someone else from spinning negative thoughts and directing them our way, we can stop the process in its tracks

If throughout the year each of us were to turn every nagging negative thought we experienced into a blessing, we would simultaneously affect the entire universal thought exchange.

by refusing to play. By simply refusing to return negative thoughts and feelings, we are neutralizing the dynamic. By neutralizing negativity we are converting the probability of an argument into the probability of civility and understanding. If throughout the year each of us were to turn every nagging negative thought we experience into a blessing, we would simultaneously affect the entire universal thought exchange. With massive participation, this effort would convert the probability of disease, destruction and war into the probability of health, peace and abundance.

If that sounds like a cosmic pipe dream, it may be because you don't understand the innate power of your own mind. Give it a try. Don't allow the unlikelihood of your neighbor's participation to deter you. It only takes one person to get the ball rolling, and I'm betting we all know exactly where to start.

26

Easter Is Not Just for Christians

To Christians of every sect, Easter is a real and sacred event, the miraculous triumph of life over death and the promise of a new and transcendent life. Although it is without question the defining moment of the Christian faith, Christians aren't the only ones who need Easter. People of all beliefs, including atheists and agnostics, have much to learn from the Easter archetype.

Contrary to popular opinion, defining a sacred event as an archetype does not relegate it to fiction. Quite the reverse. Rather, it elevates that event to mythical stature to claim its fundamental contribution to the human experience. An archetype is the original perfect prototype or design from which all like and related forms are derived. Archetypes were present in the human psyche way before religion came along.

Easter is the perfect prototype of triumph over, well, everything. Life over death. Good over evil. Love over hate. Health over sickness. Compassion and rightful action over condemnation and sin. Easter is reflected everywhere in nature and in the indomitable strength and renewal of the human spirit. It is the symbolic event outside of us and within us that transcends all spiritual, mental and material obstacles. Easter teaches us that with enough faith, commitment and courage there is no struggle we cannot meet eye-to-eye and conquer. Easter teaches us that even the most convincing appearances are often deceiving. It teaches us that there is more to life than meets the eye. That even when we think something is completely over it's really just beginning in a new form.

The archetype of Easter dominated the hospital room at my father's death years ago. Even though our human eyes and broken hearts could see that he was dying, we were simultaneously transfixed on his equally apparent birth into another form in another realm. Our father lives on. We can argue whether the resurrection of a human being manifests in physical form or spiritual form or both, but that argument is of little concern to me. Whatever form we manifest by Divine design will be the perfect form. Familiarity is rarely the way forward.

The Easter archetype is well represented by the traditional egg hunts of childhood. No matter our age, we are archetypally wired to seek the prize. Some deeper part of ourselves will always expect it. We will expect it not just because a prophet or two told us what it was and where to find it, but because the Easter archetype lives within us at the deepest level no matter our religion or intellectual beliefs, reminding us that we are more than flesh and blood. From the moment Adam's hand touched the Earth, Easter was always the plan.

This year, let's roll away the stone from the tomb of at least one crisis or trauma in our lives, rise up and move on. Become empowered.

Miracles have a way of arising when we agree to them, make room for them, and participate in their creation. Without Easter there is only death, and yet everywhere we look we see rebirth and renewal. Easter is the eternal truth available to everyone.

Life goes on.

27

Are You Creating Poverty?

Last week a remote acquaintance of mine said, "I would have read your new book by now, but I keep waiting for you to give me an autographed copy." This was a disingenuous attempt to score a free copy, I knew, and sadly, I felt my defenses rally. After all, the book took me over a year to write, and she could easily afford a hundred. In the past I'd given plenty of books away in the name of promotion or just plain generosity, but found those gestures to be largely unappreciated, and in some cases even a burden to the recipient. (*Oh my God, now I have to read this book!*) Discounted merchandise is undervalued. So I told her I'd be happy to autograph a copy when she gets one. And even though I had one in my car, I didn't give it to her.

I hoard my own books.

We are all hoarding something. I know this because we are living in a culture of stagnation and poverty so saturated that at this point we're soaked. Since we view business and government as all-powerful, we blame them first, and why not? Jobs and money are scarce. But so are courtesy, service, enthusiasm, compassion, eagerness to please, and a long list of other virtues that are not limited to the business world. Whether we withhold something as concrete as money or as abstract as gratitude, doesn't matter. When we sense a shortage of something, we hoard it. When we hoard something, it blocks the flow of give and take, buy and sell. It also blocks the natural generosity of our godly nature. And that's when things get testy.

Sticking to the business model, there's no shortage of examples. Take the airline industry, where less begets even less. Pretty soon a full-price ticket will buy us a fold-up chair in baggage. Or the banking industry, where fees mount and service recedes on a regular basis. (Does anybody know where all the coin machines went?) Or the phone industry. Or cable. I could go on. The now embedded trend is to charge more for fewer services, even though in many cases these industries are generating unprecedented profits.

In cultures of poverty, we are (individually and collectively) affected more than we realize. We draw more boundaries. There is a you and a me, but no us. Our begrudging reflex to this absence of generosity perpetuates the cycle. We become self-protective. We gather more than we need out of fear there won't be enough. As a result, there's not enough. We hoard; we withhold. We hoard things we don't even realize we're hoarding, like anger and resentment, hurling them like grenades at inappropriate and undeserving targets. We withhold compliments, assistance, and love. (We withhold books!) We use whatever deprivation we're experiencing ourselves—money, time, health, patience, or tender loving care—to justify the negative changes in our behavior. We're under pressure to pile everything up before the (imaginary) storm, failing to recognize that *we* are the storm, and our behavior fuels it.

A culture of poverty thrives in a climate of greed. We can all agree there's plenty of that. For instance, how can a business thrive long-term on the backs of highly-educated but unpaid interns? In the past, interns were paid to do the grunt work while they gained experience and exposure. Now it's standard practice for businesses to demand not just free time, but free published content, content that used to be considered intellectual property with high intrinsic value. In the medical field, hospitals thrive on the backs of doctors now strapped with massive educational debt, sky-rocketing insurance premiums, and wages lower than many hospital administrators with half the debt. But what is a hospital without its doctors? What this kind of greed produces is a disgruntled and disloyal work force that gives back as little as it gets. What suffers is the entire dynamic. Giving back as little as we get compounds restriction. Compounded restriction creates tension and angst. The sum of the parts equals not abundance, but abundant economic, emotional, and social poverty.

To end this vicious cycle, we have to understand how much we mean to each other. Not how much business means or a government's overarching policies. Business and government are reflections of what's going on with their people, you and me. They are our representatives; they reflect our collective values. The real power belongs to us, but is largely unused and grossly misunderstood. The truth is, on the most fundamental level you hold the answers to my problems and I hold the answer to yours. But that truth is useless if we don't share our talents openly. To share openly we have to figure out how to revive our generosity reflex. When we do, things will change. Families will change. Communities and corporations and even governments will change. It starts where it always starts—with the individual.

Where to begin?

A culture
of poverty
thrives
in a climate
of greed.

Ask yourself, how am I blocking the system; what do I hoard? Do I hoard compliments? Do I think someone: looks terrific, did a great job, made my life easier—and withhold praise? And if so, why? Am I afraid I'll lose something in the process? If I hoard compliments because no one ever compliments me, the way to change that is to let go of the grudge. Let the energy out of its cage and back into circulation.

Or maybe I hoard privacy, not really participating in the family or friendships or work camaraderie. If so, give it another chance. Participate graciously, one conversation or event at a time, and allow things to unfold naturally. If it's done with pure and generous intention, it will work.

Or maybe I hoard pride. Maybe I assume an attitude of superiority over my family, friends and colleagues. Or self-pity. Maybe I secretly enjoy playing the martyr, rarely allowing others to help. Or resentment. Or forgiveness. Or control.

Let it go.

As a society we like to complain about the abstract forces that constrain our lives, and there are a few that could use some finger-pointing. But the entities to which we give power are comprised of human beings. If those human beings personally adopt a conscious plan of abundance instead of poverty, they will reflect and integrate the new values of the people they represent. But first, we have to wake up and practice those values ourselves.

Cream rises.

28

10 Steps to 'Living in the Moment'

iving in the Moment has been a pop-culture catchphrase since the cultural revolution of the 1960's. It's a phrase originally borrowed from Eastern traditions that became trendy through media attention and popular courses on transcendental meditation and other spiritual practice. Now of course, it's an American mainstay. But what does it really mean? What relevance does it have in today's more hectic world? More importantly, how do we transform a catchphrase into a useful tool?

In a nutshell, to live in the moment means to be centered and focused on a single situation. Not so easy when things are not going our way, and especially when we're also being pulled in a dozen digital directions at once. People I have mentored complain that when they're in a painful situation being in the moment doesn't help, and in fact, hinders.

For instance, why would anyone choose to live fully in a moment of sheer hell? Why not drift back into the past or wander into the future for answers or comfort? But consciously or subconsciously drifting to the sentimental safety of the past or the projected safety of the future is useless and can even be dangerous. Why? Because no matter how challenged we are, any retreat is a false retreat.

Some of the challenges we experience are actually rooted in past misconceptions and assumptions that our lives should be easier than they are, or that the past was a simpler time. Or maybe we had the idea that if we followed all the rules or at least most of them, our lives would reflect order and remain under our control. In that case, we experience anything outside of that control as undeserved torment.

Or maybe we squirm out of the intense discomfort of 'the moment' by leaping frantically ahead to the future. But jumping into the future at best creates false hope and at worst, fear and anxiety, because we can do nothing about it. Our bodies can't meet our minds in this imagined future place, and our physical systems go crazy in 'fight or flight' trying to get us there. Ultimately, when an outcome is unknown, the future contains more fear than comfort.

Especially in a terrible moment we require all our resources to be intact, integrated, and at our disposal. If half our minds are wandering in the past, we have far less resource to cope. If half our minds are frozen in the fear of all that could happen, we can't possibly affect an optimal outcome. We must be fully present. To be fully present we have to call ourselves out of the past and the future and bring our minds to center. Meditation helps. Outside of rhythmic breathing, focus, and emptying our mind of thoughts, there is a particular visualization that always helps me:

1   Sit quietly in a private space.

2   Close your eyes and breathe evenly in and out for five minutes minimum.

3   Going back through the day, recall anything negative that occurred—any argument, altercation, or event perceived to be negative.

4   Visualize yourself in that place, a percentage of your spirit/energetic body having remained there.

5   Forgive yourself completely, as well as anyone else involved.

6   Do not dwell there, or spend any emotion. Remember you are not doing this to amplify the negative experience. You are doing it to extract yourself. Call your energy back and exit.

7   Visualize that energy returning within you. Feel its strength.

8   Repeat this for each negative event that has bothered you until your energy is measurably refreshed.

9   If you are not spent, go back further into the past and do the same, but not more than three incidents at once.

10   Over time and as you strengthen, you can return further back until you have forgiven/refreshed other memories, replacing them with love.

If you successfully engage in this meditation daily, you will have much more focus and resource to deal with your everyday life and the inevitable challenges that ensue. In time you will begin to understand what it truly means to be integrated and in the proverbial moment.

As an integrated being, you will experience more peace and find yourself dealing with difficult situations in a more evenhanded manner. Getting there requires daily work, but it is well worth the effort. On any given day at any given time, the only power we have is in that moment.

Don't squander it.

29

What Do Selfies, Vampires and Zombies Have in Common?

They're everywhere, right? It's impossible to leave the house without tripping over (or participating in) a selfie photo session. And back home, the airwaves are hijacked by a Halloween parade of bloodsucking vampire aristocrats and tottering zombie beasts. I can barely get through the cable guide without a transfusion. What in the narcissistic half-dead world is going on? Are we completely lost?

Or finally on our way to being found.

It would be an easy assumption to call the selfie fad narcissistic. And certainly there are more than a few selfie-obsessed people in love with their photogenics. But the great divide between our superficial lives reflected on social media and our real lives in the material world tells me that something deeper than a fad is driving this trend. Something deeper than ego or the desire to compete socially with others. Something connected to us all at a root level. Something called archetypes.

You could say selfies, vampires and zombies are joined at the archetypal hip.

I'm pretty sure the great psychiatrist and archetype pioneer, Carl Jung, would be fascinated by the images floating up on the social radar these days. Narcissists, vampires and zombies, though significant on their own, are only the tip of the current archetypal iceberg. Throw in the real-life terrorists, assassins, fundamentalist fanatics, racists, and political shapeshifters and we begin to see the full cinematic picture playing out before our eyes. Jung would no doubt interpret this as a shadow period of human consciousness. A period in which another, deeper layer of darkness, long buried, slowly surfaces from the bubbling swill of our collective unconscious, unearthing its unlovely face. A face it would never share on Twitter.

At least not yet.

Jung identified the Shadow as a primary personality archetype, universal to humankind. The Shadow represents not just darkness, as the name implies, but a fundamental split in the early human psyche. Vampires and zombies are shadow archetypes. Vampires represent immortality gained by siphoning the life force of others. Zombies represent a lack of awareness, having turned themselves over to lower forces—forces which (in real life) can include anything from impersonal corporate credos to rampant consumerism to fundamentalist dogma to unapologetic self-absorption.

The Shadow archetype is a wild thing, the dark potential within us that we fear and dare not become. Instead of burying it and tamping it down, Jung believed the Shadow must be acknowledged, met head-on, and integrated into our psyches in order to become

Perhaps this is
what the half-dead
narcissistic ghouls
are trying to tell us.
"We are an aspect
of you.
Wake up and heal."

whole—in order to wake us up so we can transform the darkness. It's no easy task, but at some point in the evolution of humanity, in order to achieve enlightenment, it must be done. Perhaps this is what the half-dead narcissistic ghouls are trying to tell us. "We are an aspect you. Wake up and heal."

The day our selfies accurately reflect our inner lives is the day we become an integrated species. This is the day the Shadow recedes and the Self of higher awareness shows up. It's a day worth waiting for. The struggle is right before us, projected on our computers, phones, TV screens and in new genres of literature dedicated to the paranormal underbelly. More than any other time in history, wrestling with the Shadow is prime time activity. Just watch the evening news. Every nighttime monster we ever feared has slipped from the shadows, parading before us in broad daylight. Terrorists with explosive backpacks, racists with rifles, enraged teens with semi-automatic weapons. Do they seek fame? Vengeance? Some kind of twisted justice?

Or just a way into the light.

Carl Jung famously said, *"Enlightenment doesn't occur from sitting around visualizing images of light, but from integrating the darker aspects of the Self into conscious personality."*

If this is true, we have much to look forward to when we are finally able to pack up our selfie sticks and subterranean archetypes and look each other in the eye without distraction. "Oh, so that's who you are!" we'll say.

"Yes, it's who I was all along."

30

How to Fulfill Your Destiny

Let's face it, destinies are hard to fulfill. First you have to know what they are, and that can take a really long time. I'm a perfect example. In 2014 I received a significant literary award for my second novel, *Mystic Tea*. There was a ceremony at the Providence, a gorgeous historic venue that previously served as a world-famous recording studio. All around me were framed discs signed by Sinatra, Lennon, Hendrix, Streisand, Stevie Wonder, Aretha Franklin and more. Bulbs flashed; applause resounded. As an author who sits in her writing cave all day, the exposure was glaring. It felt like the kind of hallucination my characters tend to have.

Prior to the award ceremony, I was interviewed on camera. The interviewer asked me many questions about my story—how I felt about the award, etc. The question that affected me most was, "What advice would you give other authors who aspire to this level of achievement?" This took a minute to process, because I certainly didn't feel the level of success they were attributing to me. But afterwards I realized that my answer applied to much more than writing. It applied to purpose and voice and the ultimate unfolding of intended destiny, not to be too grandiose.

But life can be pretty grandiose.

Let me back up a bit to a time when I wrote nonsense. Nonsense served me well and appealed to my keen sense of absurdity. I enjoyed writing it. Among other things, it cracked me up all day with the added benefit of generating a substantial income. For many years I applied the gift of nonsense to my advertising career, and did exceedingly well. But I'd known from childhood that my heart was in literary fiction, and I had to figure out a way to make that happen. So eventually I pushed advertising to the sidelines and moved fiction into the career slot.

But what to write? Since the demands of advertising had forced me to write on command, I could write about almost anything all day long. At the time, the suspense genre was selling. Of course the kind of suspense stories I enjoyed included nonsensical situations with goofy characters. So I wrote that. A little bit of comedy never hurt anyone. I continued to write short stories in the same vein with no luck. Plus, I wasn't that happy. It felt like fluff. (It was.) The writing was good, and the stories were coherent, even compelling to lovers of nonsense. But something was off. I decided to try something new.

The something new was not really new to me, but it was new to the literary world. From childhood I'd been transfixed by the stories of the mystical saints—their wild experiences in other realms. I often thought, why them? Why not us? Why not now? It never made sense to me that mystical experiences were exclusive to the distant past. If they were real, how could they be obscured by time? Also, by then I'd had rather a few of those experiences myself, which is a topic for another time. Others I knew had had similar experiences,

Each of us
is given a
unique thread,
a point-of-view,
a message
to contribute
to the story of
humankind.

some mightily more profound than mine. So it was out there. It was happening. But people weren't talking about it. Or writing about it. Or really, sharing it in any form.

The spiritual revolution of the '90's issued literary accounts of mystical phenomena in the form of nonfiction or memoir. Betty Eadie's wild bestseller, *Embraced by the Light* comes to mind. But the trend came and went. Since that aspect of human experience was what resonated most with me, I held onto it and incorporated it into my fiction. I was productive and satisfied. The only problem was that as fiction, it was genre-less. And thus void of a genre shelf, unsellable. Over the years my various agents labeled it 'metaphysical fiction' or 'mystical realism' in attempts to define it for publishers. But the traditional publishing world was not in the business of building new shelves. Some editors tried to convince their various committees that my book fit into the religion genre. It did not. Others tried to sell it as fantasy or magical realism. It was none of these.

I was not a complete marketing failure. My short stories and poetry found homes in literary journals and anthologies. And anyway, at this point, I understood that the stories I was writing mattered, at least to me. So I kept writing. This new genre, whatever it was, derived from my core. It was genuine and organic. It was my sweet spot, my authentic voice.

Which brings me to the point.

That night when the interviewer asked me what advice I would give to other writers who aspired to gold medallion literary status, I said, "Be true to your own voice, no matter what." It sounds a bit lofty, I know. But it is truth. Each of us is given a unique thread, a point-of-view, a message to contribute to the story of humankind. Somewhere deep down, we know what it is, but too often we sell out for one reason or another. Some of those reasons are legitimate;

i.e., survival. We have families to support. Which is not to say that the voice couldn't be developed during off-hours. It could. And furthermore, it must.

Whether the story thread or voice you've been entrusted with is in the field of literature, medicine, military, teaching, or circus performance, doesn't matter. What matters is that you pursue it to understand who you are. Once you understand this, you will know what to do with it. Furthermore, you will know that it is an essential and unique aspect of the human tapestry. You will know that humanity can't do without it. You must express it. If not you, then who?

If that slim filament, that fugitive Idea that was entrusted to you or me is not developed, even a little, it will likely disappear. But if you develop it in spite of the mighty forces that work against you, what then? Will it work? Or will it be an extravagant waste of time? Will you die in obscurity? You might. I have died a thousand deaths already in my so-called career. My obscurity was so dense at times I barely recognized myself in the mirror. On the other hand, maybe you'll beat your head against the wall of resistance long enough to bring the wall down. Once you do, you have accomplished that feat not only for yourself, but for others. Others whose paths will be that much easier because of your efforts. Everybody wins. Destinies are fulfilled.

And who knows, maybe you'll even win an award.

31

Who Don't You Love?

By all accounts and in all religions, we are called to love each other. We are in fact told over and over again that there is no OTHER. There is only ONE and it encompasses us all. Armed with that beneficent arsenal of sound advice and good will, we nevertheless pick and choose our company, sometimes even our neighbors, to suit ourselves. In the end, we opt mostly for those who operate well within our political, racial, religious, social and personal comfort zones. Those who don't challenge our belief systems may be easier to love, but ironically, they don't teach us much about love.

Real love looks outside itself.

I have a friend who is a pastor at a local church who takes in the homeless every night. Other pastors of other denominations in the same area have refused sanctuary to these chronic homeless because they seemingly make no attempt to better themselves. "We can't afford it," they say. "We have to take care of our own parishioners." My friend doesn't see it that way. He says, "I don't know what a homeless person looks like, but I know what a human being looks like." So he takes them in. He feeds them and gives them shelter. He sees God in them, and they no doubt see God in him.

The practice of compassion doesn't have to start with the homeless or others radically outside our circles. Many of us don't even practice compassion with those we love, or used to love, whose situations have changed. The friend with a devastating diagnosis, the aunt with Alzheimer's, the cousin with the autistic child, the irritable elderly neighbor, the family down the block suffering so much devastation from the loss of a child that we ourselves can't face them for fear of saying the wrong thing. Their situations make us uncomfortable. So we hide.

The list of sorrows confronting us through the lives of others is sometimes so endless and overwhelming that in the end, we do nothing at all. These situations and these people cross our minds; we may even pray for them, but in the end we don't do what they need us to do. We don't act. For whatever reason, (name the excuse), we never get around to making the phone call, paying the visit, sending the card, dropping off the meal. Instead of reaching out, we move further into our own womb of comfort and validation until we're the ones kicked out by the alienating centripetal force of disease, bankruptcy, imprisonment or any other situation that invites unwarranted shame or devastation upon us or our inner circle. And then we say, "Why me?"

When pondering the many such alienating scenarios I have survived, I realize that the situations that present themselves to us through others are not accidental. They are intended as much or more for us as they are for the people in the eye of a

Until we love
outside of our own
comfort zones,
we haven't really
loved at all.

particular storm. Think of each of these scenarios as a hand-engraved, personalized invitation to love with a capital "L"—to act with compassion. In my own life, I can tell you that the more discomfort I felt in a situation that called for love, the more I ultimately learned from it. Until we love outside of our own comfort zones, we haven't really loved at all. Until we have allowed that kind of love to change us, to expand our boundaries and redefine us, we don't even know what love is. Love within our own comfort zones is convenient, conditional, and more like self-love than the divine agape love we are ultimately called upon to express to each other.

We hear much talk from pulpits about the Coming of the Kingdom of God, but that Kingdom will most likely not be descending upon us like some magical spinning sun. It will arise from within. It will arise from a place of compassion that we have (hopefully) created and prepared in our hearts. A place we have nurtured and developed not by some distant ideal, but by intentional and deliberate action.

How to develop this gift? Start by finding a place in your heart for one person who makes you uncomfortable. Reach out to them and feel your discomfort; feel theirs. Be okay with any awkwardness that arises. This is the breeding ground of change and growth. Allow that growth to change you, to carve room for others in your heart. Each place you create makes room for another, and on and on.

Compassion is a muscle. It won't develop without use.

Who we love says something about us, but who we don't love says more. The good news is, with a little effort, we can shorten that list.

32

How to Put the Power in Prayer

I've prayed for a lot of people in my life, and I've been well prayed for too. Some of it worked out and some of it did not, or so it seemed. When things did not work out, the result was generally greeted by others with a flurry of excuses, such as, 'It wasn't meant to be,' or 'God's ways are mysterious.' Firm in the belief that meaningful prayer should produce a result, however, I pushed through some of that mystery, improving the odds.

In the simplest terms, prayer is intention. Intention is focused thought. In prayer, we lift our intention consciously into the universe, generally directed at God, or in some cases, a divine intermediary whose job it is to amplify that intention and send it on up to the head office. Prayer has always had a mystique about it, placing it in the unearthly category of the magical unknown. It's true that when prayers are answered, it's pretty magical. But it's also true that, thanks to modern physics, some of the mystery can be explained in scientific terms.

Prayer may rise up from the heart, but it's generally articulated through the brain and moves into the universe in waves. Brain waves are forms of electromagnetic radiation that, like other electromagnetic waves, travel at the speed of light. Depending on their strength, waves have the power to affect the energy and objects in their path. Since brain waves are not as strong as other electromagnetic waves, they benefit from fortification. This may be one reason why prayer works best in groups of two or more. Groups of people compassionately directing intention with the same focus on the same object, create a stronger wave that's more likely to effect the desired change. Large groups of people focusing on a unified outcome have tremendous potential for significant impact.

The first time I saw this process actualized, it sent me to my knees.

The year was 2008. Our son was gravely ill, and the doctors told my husband and me that he would likely not survive the night. That was the eve of his nineteenth birthday. On the surface this appeared to be the tragic climax of an arduous three-year-long war against blood cancer. There were those in our circles who piously accepted this prognosis as God's will. "At least you had those three years," they said. "You'll always be grateful for that."

I wasn't the least bit grateful.

As a magical thinker and deep spiritual believer, I wanted my son not only to survive, but to thrive. He was an incredibly intelligent, clever, and motivated young man with a great deal more to offer his family and the world. As his spiritual and medical advocate, I was intractable in the belief that God could save him if he wanted to. *Just do it! Why aren't you doing it?!* It pained me to ask, because after all, couldn't he read my mind? My prayers were bold, honest, and combative. I had nothing to lose. I was a spiritual lioness defending her cub. The doctors had done all they could. I was waiting on a God who was taking his sweet time.

But what if he was waiting on me?

Saint Paul and other mystics talk about the *'Mystical Body'* as more or less the eyes, ears, arms and legs, etc. of God on Earth. Infused with latent divinity, we are charged with tuning our antenna, balancing our psyches, and developing these spiritual gifts at all cost.

"These things and more will you do in my name." — John 13:13

For the foot soldiers among us, this may mean feeding the hungry and sheltering the homeless. For those whose gifts derive from mystical realms, it may mean learning how to manifest outright miracles. One thing is true, as the collective mystical body, we are endowed with more power than we've ever bothered to develop. It makes sense that at some point in human evolution God would kick us out of the nest and let us figure it out for ourselves. How else does one learn to fly?

"Ask and you shall receive. Seek and you shall find.
Knock and the door will be opened." — Matthew 7:7

At the peak of my son's jeopardy, I thought I grasped the power of petition. But in the midst of that experience, I was shown an order of prayer higher than I believed possible. That night as he struggled so profoundly, I called my family and widespread prayer community, soliciting support. Those who were not wringing their hands with anxiety, got down to business recruiting more prayer groups through friends and over the internet, on and on, until a chain of viral prayer swept the globe, gathering speed and force in a fast-moving tsunami of advocacy for our child. The numbers were overwhelming, and included over fifteen countries. The intention was strong and direct. *"Save him,"* said the wave. "Let it be done."

Early the following morning, I awoke with a start, instantly aware of a major shift. Against all evidence to the contrary, I knew my son had been healed. *I knew it.* I had never experienced such a *knowing* in my entire life. I rushed to his side, where he was struggling beneath his oxygen mask. The nurse said she would call the doctor, that the infiltrate in his lungs was overwhelming him. We would have to make decisions. Things had taken a turn for the worse.

"No," I said. "Lift the mask. He's trying to tell us something."

She protested, but consumed with pity, I suppose, pulled his mask aside to prove her point. As soon as the mask was off, he sang 'Happy Birthday' to himself, smiling; his eyes clear and alert. Considering his acute level of infection, just the ability to breathe on his own would have stunned the nurse. But the ability to sing was otherworldly. Doctors ordered a mobile x-ray, which proved the infiltrate had all but disappeared. He was moved out of ICU later that day. The next morning he walked down the hall and took a shower on his own. Two days later, he was back in his college dorm.

He hasn't been sick since.

What I want people to know from this experience is that every prayer matters. Not the lazy drive-by prayers tossed blindly into a black hole. You know the ones. Not those. Not the anxious prayers fueled by fear and desperation. Put those prayers away. Those prayers are for the spiritually undeveloped. It's time to learn the confident prayers of empowered believers, the kind that rise up from the indwelling of the divinity at the core of your being and mine. The future of the world depends on this. It is our evolutionary responsibility to develop these gifts. Every selfless thought and intention directed confidently at the healing of another person,

Every selfless thought and intention ...stacks the deck in favor of survival and enlightenment.

animal, plant, or the Earth itself, stacks the deck in favor of survival and enlightenment. Every prayer counts.

How to begin?

1   When someone requests prayer, pray for them instantly, fervently, and confidently.

2   Form what I call 'a ring of commitment' around their intention. Reject all temptation towards fear and doubt. Your job now is to pray against the tide. Loosed of the burden of earthly logic, you are empowered to unleash your considerable energetic force into the wave of possibility that will likely turn that tide in favor of the intention.

3   In between prayer requests, pray, meditate, and generally commit to your own spiritual development. After all, your prayer could be the tipping point, not only of an individual's recovery, but a community's. Or a nation's. Or the Earth.

Or the spiritual empowerment of humankind.

ABOUT THE AUTHOR

Rea Nolan Martin is the award-winning author of three novels: *Mystic Tea, The Anesthesia Game* and *The Sublime Transformation of Vera Wright.*

She has published numerous essays, short stories and poems in literary journals and anthologies. *Walking on Water* is her first book-length work of nonfiction.

35752603R00096

Made in the USA
San Bernardino, CA
04 July 2016